Aroma Rice Cooker Cookbook

Easy and Delicious Rice Cooker Recipes for the Whole Family

Brice Watson

Copyright © 2010 by Brice Watson

All rights reserved worldwide.

ISBN: 978-1670007568

No part of this book may be reproduced or transmitted in any form or by any means, electronic or mechanical, including photocopying, recording or by any information storage and retrieval system, without written permission from the publisher, except for the inclusion of brief quotations in a review.

Warning-Disclaimer

The purpose of this book is to educate and entertain. The author or publisher does not guarantee that anyone following the techniques, suggestions, ideas, or strategies will become successful. The author and publisher shall have neither liability or responsibility to anyone with respect to any loss or damage caused, or alleged to be caused, directly or indirectly by the information contained in this book.

CONTENTS

Introduction 4

Aroma Rice Cooker and Food Steamer 5

Chapter 1
    Rice and Other Grains 11

Chapter 2
    Poultry, Beef, Seafood and Pork 54

Chapter 3
    Vegetable and Side Dishes Recipes 67

Chapter 4
    Soups, Stews and Chilies 80

Chapter 5
    Desserts 94

Conclusion 107

INTRODUCTION

Aroma Rice Cooker and Food Steamer is the perfect kitchenware for someone who is busy and always on the go. No more waiting for the boiling of the rice, and you don't have to stir it constantly. You can have perfect rice with the Aroma Rice Cooker. Not only do you have the advantage of perfect rice, but you also can cook other dishes with it. The cooking options of this cooker allow you to cook your whole dish. The programmed and "keep warm" controls make you more efficient in cooking. Now you can cook meals in one piece of cookware with no hassle.

Stop dragging out your pots and pans because Aroma Rice Cooker and Food Steamer is all that you need. This rice cooker and food steamer are very easy to use. It is considered to be a multi-functional rice cooker since it has different features that you can use in cooking variety of dishes. It can cook rice, but also a wide range of different dishes like quinoa, oatmeal, meats and vegetables.

It can definitely save you time by learning easy to cook recipes using Aroma Rice Cooker and Food Steamer. This cookbook is loaded with healthy recipes and delicious meals that you can prepare and cook easily in a short period. Put everything in the cooker and wait briefly. You can spend more time on more important things like bonding with your family. So get yourself ready as we share with you these healthy recipes that you can cook for your family.

Create great memories with your family at the same time that you are cooking perfect food for them using Aroma Rice Cooker and Food Steamer. Explore and be in love with this cooker as we tell you a little bit more about it. You'll be impressed by how much this cooker can do. It can really make more than just rice.

AROMA RICE COOKER AND FOOD STEAMER

Aroma Rice Cooker and Food Steamer is made by Aroma Housewares Company, a leading American brand for rice cookers. They are known for providing cookware and kitchen appliances that enhance and enrich their customers' lives. The design of this cooker is perfect for everybody. It is a necessity in everyone's kitchen because of everything that it can offer from cooking rice to preparing your family's main course.

As mentioned, you can make and prepare healthy meals and vegetable sides using this type of rice cooker. This cooker has different multi-function specially designed for your needs.

- **White Rice** – Cooks delicious white rice automatically. The waiting time will depend on the amount of rice that you are cooking. The greater the number of cups, the longer it cooks.

- **Brown Rice** – This is perfect not only for brown rice, but for other grains that require more time to cook or grains that are tough to cook.

- **Steam** – This setting is used for vegetable sides and main courses. You just have to set the timer. Once it reaches a boil, the countdown will begin. It will automatically shut off once the countdown is over.

- **Slow Cook** – Ideal for cooking homemade stews and roasts. You can set the timer from 2 to 8 hours depending on the time you need in cooking your healthy meals.

- **Flash Rice** – Time-saving option for rice in a pinch. It will cut 50% of your cooking time.

- **Keep Warm** – Once rice is cooked, it will automatically turn to "keep warm" mode. This function will keep your food warm and ready to serve.

- **Delay Timer** – This function is ideal for cooking rice when you need it to be cooked. For instance, you set it to be cooked in 6 hours, the cooker function will just activate in 6 hours. Prepare the uncooked rice in the morning and cooked rice will be ready when you get home.

How does it work?

Aroma Rice Cooker and Food Steamer is America's No. 1 Rice Cooker. It's no wonder because it is easy to use and so convenient. All of its digital controls are very useful in everyday cooking. But how does it really work and what are the precautions that you need to consider?

When using it for the first time, be sure to read all the instruction in the manual for your own safety. It is essential to remove all the packaging materials, especially the plastic bags because it is hazardous for children. Before using it, wash the accessories and inner pot in warm soapy water and rinse it thoroughly. Dry thoroughly. With a damp cloth, wipe the body of the cooker clean.

Remember that you should not immerse the rice cooker base, cord or plug in water to protect from electrical shock. It's also advisable that you place it away from gas stoves, ovens and electric burner. In cooking rice, remember the 1:1 ratio. One cup of uncooked rice needs one cup of water. So if you are going to cook 3 cups of rice, you need 3 cups of water. Rinse the water inside the pot to remove excess starch, then add the appropriate amount of water.

Take note that white rice should soak for 10 to 20 minutes before cooking, whereas brown rice and other tough grains need more time. Close the lid of the cooker and plug to 120V AC outlet. Then press the power button. After that press the White Rice or Brown Rice depending on the type of rice you are cooking. The cooker will start cooking your rice and you will notice an indicator light. Once the rice is cooked, the control will automatically change to Keep Warm mode. Always turn off the cooker and unplug it after use.

Below is the Rice Measurement Table that you can use as a reference when cooking white rice, brown rice or other grains.

RICE MEASUREMENT TABLE

Uncooked Rice	**Rice Water Line Inside Pot**	**Cooking Times**
2 Cups	Line 2	White Rice: 27-32 Min. Brown Rice: 41-46 Min.
3 Cups	Line 3	White Rice: 32-37 Min. Brown Rice: 43-48 Min
4 Cups	Line 4	White Rice: 35-39 Min. Brown Rice: 45-50 Min.
5 Cups	Line 5	White Rice: 36-41 Min. Brown Rice: 48-53 Min.
6 Cups	Line 6	White Rice: 37-45 Min. Brown Rice: 51-56 Min.
7 Cups	Line 7	White Rice: 40-48 Min. Brown Rice: 51-56 Min.
8 Cups	Line 8	White Rice: 40-48 Min. Brown Rice: 52-57 Min.
9 Cups	Line 9	White Rice: 41-46 Min. Brown Rice: 54-59 Min.
10 Cups	Line 10	White Rice: 41-46 Min. Brown Rice: 55-60 Min.

Of course you can always use the Flash Rice option every time you are in a hurry. You can save 50% of your cooking time for both white and brown rice.

It is also effortless to steam using this Aroma Cooker. Just put some water in the pot. Your water level will depend on the type of food that you are cooking. After adding some water, place it to the cooker. Prepare food to be steamed in the steam tray and place it to the cooker. Close the lid of the cooker and plug to 120V AC outlet, then press the power button. After that you can press the Steam button. It will display a "5" which means 5 minutes of steam time. You can adjust it by pressing (-) or (+). Once the water reaches its boil, the countdown of the timer will start. Just like in cooking rice, it will turn to Keep Warm when the countdown is down to zero.

Below is the Steaming Table that you can use as a reference when cooking meat and vegetables.

STEAMING TABLE

Meat/Vegetable	Amount of Water	Steaming Time
Fish	2 Cups	25 Mins.
Chicken	2 ½ Cups	30 Mins.
Pork	2 ½ Cups	30 Mins
Beef	2 ½ Cups	Medium = 25 Min. Medium-Well = 30 Min. Well = 33 Min.
Asparagus	¾ Cup	20 Mins.
Broccoli	½ Cup	15 Mins.
Cabbage	1 Cup	25 Mins.
Carrots	1 Cup	25 Mins.

Cauliflower	1 Cup	25 Mins.
Corn	1 Cup	25 Mins.
Eggplant	1¼ Cups	30 Mins.
Green Beans	1 Cup	15 Mins.
Peas	¾ Cup	20 Mins
Spinach	¾ Cup	20 Mins
Squash	¾ Cup	20 Mins
Zucchini	¾ Cup	20 Mins

Steaming time will always depend on the cut of the meat or vegetables that you use. Remember to always close the lid and allow for some time before opening the lid after steaming to avoid the escape of hot steam that could cause you burns.

Advantages of Having An Aroma Rice Cooker and Food Steamer

There are a lot of benefits in having Aroma Rice Cooker and Food Steamer. It is like all-in-one kitchenware that is very useful for you and your family. You can cook rice perfectly, reduce your food bill, keep your kitchen cooler, increase the nutritional value of your food, and save your time.

- **Cooks rice perfectly** – A lot of people have problems cooking rice because of the effort you have to exert when cooking it. Imagine stirring endlessly until it gets cooked so the rice won't stick to the bottom of the pot. You really need to dedicate some time to make perfect rice, but with this cooker, you can prepare and measure the uncooked rice and water and just do whatever you need to do.

- **Reduces food bill** – There comes a time that the rice is not cooked enough or it is overcooked and we just throw it away. Not anymore! Not if you have a Rice Cooker! You just have to time the cooking and wait for the sound of your timer. No more wasted food and wasted money.

- **Keeps kitchen cooler** – Compared to traditional cooking, this cooker produce less heat to the kitchen environment making it cooler. It is most helpful during summer when it is so hot.

- **Increases nutritional value** – Aroma Rice Cooker and Food Steamer is perfect for health-oriented diets such as raw food diet, Okinawa diet and macrobiotic diet since you can cook food with less oil or no oil at all.

- **Time saver** – With this cooker, you can steam vegetables while cooking rice. It is perfect for the mom on-the-go and for people who are busy. You just have to put the vegetables in the steamer and place the steamer over the rice. Once the rice is cooked, you can rest assured that the vegetables are ready to eat.

You will surely love your new kitchenware, the Aroma Rice Cooker and Food Steamer because of what it can do for you. Do not settle for less because you deserve the best. Own this cooker and be in love with it as it will make your life stress-free. You will realize that preparing food has never been so easy.

This Aroma Rice Cooker Cookbook has a lot of healthy recipes to choose from. Enjoy as you learn new recipes and techniques in cooking.

CHAPTER 1
RICE AND OTHER GRAINS

Strawberry Goldilocks Porridge

Servings: 4 | Prep Time: 5 minutes | Cooking Time: 10 minutes

Ingredients

- 1 cup brown rice farina
- 1 cup low-fat milk
- ½ cup strawberries, sliced
- ¼ cup sour cream
- 2 tablespoons honey
- 2 cups water
- 1 pinch brown sugar

Directions

1. Add farina to the rice cooker. Stir in milk and 2 cups of water.
2. Close the lid, press the STEAM button, and cook for 10 minutes.
3. Open the lid after 5 minutes and give it a good stir.
4. Once cooking is complete, carefully open the rice cooker's lid, keeping hands and face away to avoid steam burns.
5. Divide the porridge between 4 bowls.
6. Top with strawberries, sour cream and honey.
7. Drizzle with brown sugar and serve.

Nutrition Values (Per Serving)

Calories: 385 Fat 12g Carbohydrates: 48g Protein: 7g

Bacon Mushroom Risotto

Servings: 6 | Prep Time: 10 minutes | Cooking Time: 30-40 minutes

Ingredients

2 teaspoons olive oil
2 Portobello mushrooms, sliced into 1 inch pieces
Salt and pepper to taste
2 garlic cloves, minced
4 ½ cups vegetable broth
2 ½ cups white wine
1 cup Arborio rice
1 pinch of dried basil
¼ cup Parmesan cheese, grated
¼ cup Romano cheese, grated
¼ cup heavy cream
6 strips bacon, cooked crispy and crumbled

Directions

1. Set your Aroma Cooker to STEAM mode and heat oil for 5 minutes.
2. Add in mushrooms, salt, pepper and stir. Cook until tender, for about 3-4 minutes. Stir in garlic and cook for 1 more minute.
3. Pour 1 cup of broth and ½ cup of white wine. Give it a good stir.
4. Add rice, basil and season with a pinch of salt and pepper.
5. Stir well, close the lid, and cook until the liquid has been absorbed.
6. Carefully open the lid and add another cup of broth and ½ cup white wine.
7. Keep stirring until the liquid is absorbed again. The whole process should take around 30-40 minutes.
8. Once tender, add cheese and season with salt and pepper again. Stir in bacon and heavy cream, and serve in bowls garnished with more bacon.

Nutrition Values (Per Serving)

Calories: 354 Fat: 18g Carbohydrates: 25g Protein: 12g

Brown Rice Tabbouleh

Servings: 4 | Prep Time: 10 minutes | Cooking Time: 35 -40 minutes

Ingredients

1 ½ cups medium-grain brown rice
2 cups water
½ a teaspoon salt
2 small tomatoes, ripe, cut into small cubes
1 ½ cup European cucumber, cut into small cubes
1 ½ cup green onion, minced
⅛ cup mint leaves, chopped
⅛ cup extra virgin olive oil
1 tablespoon lemon juice
1 pinch paprika
Salt and pepper to taste

Directions

1. Rinse the rice under cold water and drain, then transfer to your Aroma Cooker.
2. Add water and season with salt.
3. Give it a gentle stir and close the lid.
4. Press BROWN RICE and let the cooking cycle complete.
5. When ready, open the lid and fluff the rice with a fork.
6. Transfer the rice to a large plate and let it sit for 30 minutes.
7. Take another bowl and mix in the remaining ingredients.
8. Season with salt and pepper.
9. Once the rice is cool, add the previously prepared mixture to the rice and toss well to mix everything up.
10. Serve and enjoy!

Nutrition Values (Per Serving)

Calories: 267 Fat: 12g Carbohydrates: 37g Protein: 5g

Vegetables Rice

Servings: 6 | Prep Time: 10 minutes | Cooking Time: 35 -40 minutes

Ingredients

- 2 tablespoons unsalted butter
- ¼ cup carrots, sliced in rounds
- 1 ½ cups long-grain white rice
- 2 cups vegetable stock
- 1 tablespoon fresh Italian parsley, chopped
- 1 teaspoon dried thyme
- ¼ cup frozen peas
- 1 tablespoon chopped almonds

Directions

1. Take a small skillet and place it over medium heat.
2. Melt 1 tablespoon of butter and add carrots, stirring occasionally for 2-3 minutes.
3. In the meantime, add rice to your Aroma cooker.
4. Stir in stock, thyme, parsley, peas and the sautéed carrots.
5. Close the lid and cook on WHITE RICE mode.
6. Once the cooking cycle is over, the cooker will switch to WARM mode.
7. Let it sit for 10 minutes, then carefully open the lid.
8. Fluff the rice and stir in 1 tablespoon of butter and almonds.
9. Serve immediately.

Nutrition Values (Per Serving)

Calories: 212 Fat: 5g Carbohydrates: 32g Protein: 15g

Ultimate Orange Chipotle Risotto

Servings: 4 | Prep Time: 10 minutes | Cooking Time: 35-45 minutes

Ingredients

1 tablespoon butter
1 cup small onion, diced
1 cup Arborio rice
3 cups hot water
1 cup orange juice
Zest from ½ orange
1 teaspoon saffron thread, optional
1 chipotle chile in adobo
3 ounces asiago cheese + ½ cup grated asiago cheese
¼ cup freshly chopped parsley

Directions

1. Set your Aroma Cooker to STEAM mode and melt butter.
2. Stir in the onions and sauté for 2-3 minutes until translucent.
3. Add the rice, water, orange juice, saffron, zest, chipotle pepper and saffron.
4. Close the lid and cook on BROWN RICE mode until the cooking cycle is over.
5. When the rice cooker switches to warm mode, carefully open the lid, and sprinkle with freshly grated cheese and herbs.
6. Season with salt and pepper, give it a good stir and serve.

Nutrition Values (Per Serving)

Calories: 321 Fat: 9g Carbohydrates: 46g Protein: 13g

Fragrant Basmati Rice

Servings: 3 | Prep Time: 15 minutes | Cooking Time: 35-45 minutes

Ingredients

- 1 cup basmati rice
- 1 ½ cups water
- ¼ teaspoon salt
- 1 cinnamon stick (4 inches)
- 3 green cardamom pods

Directions

1. Rinse the rice and drain. Add the listed ingredients and the rice to your Aroma cooker.
2. Give it a good stir and close the lid. Cook on WHITE RICE mode and allow the cooking cycle to complete.
3. Once it goes off, the cooker will automatically switch to WARM mode.
4. Keep on WARM mode for 15 minutes, lid closed.
5. After 15 minutes, carefully open the lid.
6. Fluff and serve into serving bowls.

Nutrition Values (Per Serving)

Calories: 275 Fat: 4g Carbohydrates: 45g Protein: 5g

Generic Brown Rice

Servings: 8 | Prep Time: 5 minutes | Cooking Time: 65-75 minutes

Ingredients

- 2 cups brown rice, rinsed and drained
- Water to fill up to line 2
- Butter for greasing
- Salt to taste

Directions

1. Grease the inner pot and add the rice. Season with salt. Fill the inner pot with water up to line 2. Swirl well and close the lid.
2. Cook on BROWN RICE mode until the cycle completes and the rice cooker goes to WARM mode. Let it sit for 10 minutes.
3. Fluff the rice and serve.

Nutrition Values (Per Serving)

Calories: 174 Fat: 1g Carbohydrates: 37g Protein: 4g

Sesame Chicken Rice

Servings: 6 | Prep Time: 10 minutes | Cooking Time: 35 minutes

Ingredients

- 2 tablespoons peanut oil
- 1 teaspoon sesame oil
- 1 tablespoon finely grated fresh ginger
- 2 garlic cloves, peeled and crushed
- 2 onions, peeled and sliced
- 2 cups short grain rice
- 2 cups cooked chicken, chopped
- ¼ cup shallots, chopped
- 2 tablespoons sesame seeds, toasted
- 3 cups chicken stock

Directions

1. Set your Aroma Cooker to STEAM mode and set timer to 5 minutes.
2. Heat the oils, and add in ginger, onions and garlic. Stir-fry for 2 minutes.
3. Add the washed rice, stir and cook for another minute.
4. Pour chicken stock and close the lid. Press WHITE RICE and let the cycle complete. Once it goes off, open the lid and mix in chicken, sesame seeds and shallots.
5. Close the lid and let it simmer in WARM mode for 10 minutes before serving.

Nutrition Values (Per Serving)

Calories: 422 Fat: 27g Carbohydrates: 62g Protein: 32g

Red Ruby Beans And Rice

Servings: 6 | Prep Time: 10 minutes | Cooking Time: 25-35 minutes

Ingredients

1 cup white rice
1 ¼ cups water
1 ½ teaspoons cumin
2 teaspoons salt
3 teaspoons chili powder
1 ½ teaspoons garlic powder
¾ teaspoon paprika
1 bell pepper, finely diced
1 onion, finely diced
½ pound ham, diced
1 can red kidney beans, drained and rinsed

Directions

1. Add rice, water, bell pepper, onions and spices to your Aroma cooker.
2. Stir and close the lid. Push the WHITE RICE button and start the cooking cycle.
3. After 10 minutes, open the lid, stir in ham and close the lid.
4. Let the cycle finish and wait for the cooker to switch to WARM mode.
5. Open the lid and let it sit for 5-10 minutes.
6. Serve and enjoy!

Nutrition Values (Per Serving)

Calories: 328 Fat: 10g Carbohydrates: 23g Protein: 23g

Sweet Corn and Wild Rice

Servings: 4 | Prep Time: 5 minutes | Cooking Time: 25-30 minutes

Ingredients

¼ cup fresh parsley, minced
¼ pound baby carrots, skins scrubbed, tops trimmed
¼ pound baby corn on cobs, rinsed
Pinch kosher salt

Rice Ingredients

2 cups vegetable broth
1 ½ cups uncooked wild rice, rinsed and soaked in 2 cups water for 30 minutes
1 cup Green Beans, ends and stringy bits removed, sliced into ½-inch long slivers
1 can 15-ounce cannelloni beans
1 can 15-ounce diced tomatoes
1 can 15-ounce whole kernel sweet corn, rinsed
Dash black pepper
Dash kosher salt
Water

Directions

1. Place carrots and corn in your steamer tray.
2. Season with salt and set aside.
3. Add all ingredients listed under the rice to your rice cooker and stir.
4. Pour just enough water to reach the level 4 mark.
5. Place steam tray on top.
6. Close the lid, push the BROWN RICE button and let the cooking cycle complete.
7. Once ready, the cooker will automatically switch to WARM mode.
8. Open the lid and drain vegetables.
9. Serve garnished with fresh parsley and a portion steamed veggies

Nutrition Values (Per Serving)

Calories: 247 Fat: 11g Carbohydrates: 34g Protein: 7g

Easy To Make Lime Cilantro Dish

Servings: 4 | Prep Time: 10 minutes | Cooking Time: 35 minutes

Ingredients

2 cups of white rice, long-grain washed
2 teaspoons olive oil
1 lime zest and juice of ½ lime
2 tablespoons fresh cilantro, minced
1 teaspoon salt

Directions

1. Take a skillet and place it over medium-low heat.
2. Add rice and oil and stir-fry for 5 minutes.
3. Transfer the toasted rice to your Aroma Cooker and add water to level 2 mark.
4. Close the lid, press WHITE RICE and cook until the cooking cycle completes.
5. Once done, open the lid and fluff the rice.
6. Transfer to a serving bowl and add lime juice, zest and cilantro.

Nutrition Values (Per Serving)

Calories: 247 Fat: 10g Carbohydrates: 27g Protein: 12g

Authentic Spanish Rice

Servings: 8 | Prep Time: 10 minutes (TO MOVE BACK) | Cooking Time: 35 minutes

Ingredients

2 cups long-grain white rice
2 cups water
1 (8 ounce) can tomato sauce
14 ounces Mexican Style stewed tomatoes, with juice
¼ cup salsa
¾ teaspoon cumin
¾ teaspoon garlic salt
2 teaspoons chili powder
1 ½ teaspoons dried onion
¾ teaspoon salt
1 small green pepper, diced
1 can diced green chilies, optional

Directions

1. Grease the inner pot of your Aroma cooker with cooking spray.
2. Add the rice and 2 cups of water along with the other ingredients and stir well.
3. Close the lid, push the WHITE RICE button, and near the end of the cooking cycle check if the rice is cooked properly. If not, cook it until the desired consistency.
4. Once the Aroma Cooker switches to WARM mode, let it sit for 5 minutes.
5. Carefully open the lid and serve.

Nutrition Values (Per Serving)

Calories: 328 Fat: 6g Carbohydrates: 58g Protein: 8g

Very "Wild" Rice

Servings: 8 | Prep Time: 5 minutes | Cooking Time: 65-75 minutes

Ingredients

2 cups wild rice, rinsed and drained
4 cups unsalted chicken stock
Butter for grease
Salt to taste

Directions

1. Grease the inner cooking pot with butter. Add the rice and season with salt.
2. Fill the cooker with water up to line 2 mark. Stir and close the lid.
3. Push the BROWN RICE button and let the cooking cycle complete.
4. Once the Aroma Pot switches to WARM mode, let the rice simmer for 10 minutes. After that, fluff the rice and transfer to serving bowls.

Nutrition Values (Per Serving)

Calories: 200 Fat: 2g Carbohydrates: 36g Protein: 10g

Thai Prawn with Peas Fried Rice

Servings: 4-6 | Prep Time: 5 minutes | Cooking Time: 40 minutes

Ingredients

2 tablespoons oil
1 medium onion, halved and thinly sliced
2 garlic cloves, minced
1 red hot chili, chopped
2 cups brown rice, soaked and drained
1 cup raw prawns, peeled and deveined
Water, to fill up to line 2
½ cup canned peas, drained
1 tablespoon light soy sauce
1 tablespoon fish sauce
½ cup loosely packed fresh coriander, chopped
4 large whole eggs, beaten
Hot chili sauce to taste

Directions

1. Drain the soaked rice for 2 hours prior to cooking. Add water to your inner pot up to line 2. Place the inner pot in the rice cooker and add rice.
2. Give it a good stir and close the lid. Cook on BROWN RICE and allow the cooking cycle to complete.
3. Once done, let the rice sit for 10 minutes and remove the lid. Fluff it and transfer to a bowl. Wash the inner pot and place it back to your cooker.
4. Press BROWN RICE and wait for a few minutes to heat up.
5. Add oil and the beaten eggs, fry until lightly browned. Flip and fry for 1 minute more.
6. Remove the fried eggs from the inner pot and let cool, then chop the eggs into small pieces. Pour 1 tablespoon of oil to the pot and heat.
7. Add garlic and chili and sauté for 1-2 minutes or until fragrant. Stir in the prawns and cook for 2-3 minutes until opaque.

8. Next, stir in peas and rice, and season with salt and pepper. Stir in ¾ parts of coriander and cook for 3 minutes.
9. When ready, remove and serve with eggs, prawns and onion mix. Top the rice with coriander and chili sauce and serve.

Nutrition Values (Per Serving)

Calories: 358 Fat: 16g Carbohydrates: 42g Protein: 10g

Amazing Ginger and Chicken Rice

Servings: 4 | Prep Time: 10 minutes | Cooking Time: 45 minutes

Ingredients

1 large chicken bouillon cube
¾ cup hot water
1 cup jasmine rice
1 ¼ pounds skinless, boneless chicken thighs cut into 1-inch cubes
1 2-inch piece of fresh ginger, peeled and cut into matchsticks
3 packed cups baby spinach
1 cup unsweetened coconut milk
Salt to taste

Directions

1. Take a small bowl with hot water and dissolve bouillon cube.
2. Add rice, chicken and ginger to your Aroma Cooker.
3. Arrange spinach on top and pour in the coconut milk and bouillon broth. Salt to taste.
4. Close the lid, push the WHITE RICE button, and let the cooking cycle complete.
5. Once the cooker switches to WARM mode, let it sit for 5 minutes with the lid closed. Open the lid and fluff the rice with a fork before serving.

Nutrition Values (Per Serving)

Calories: 467 Fat: 29g Carbohydrates: 11g Protein: 38g

Beautiful Lemon Rice

Servings: 4 | Prep Time: 5 minutes | Cooking Time: 30-40 minutes

Ingredients

1 cup long-grain white rice
1 ½ cups vegetable stock
1 pinch salt
1 large garlic clove

Zest of ½ lemon, freshly grated
2 tablespoons unsalted butter
2 tablespoons fresh Italian parsley

Directions

1. Add the rice, stock and salt to your Aroma cooker. Stir and top with garlic.
2. Close the lid, select WHITE RICE and let the cooking cycle complete.
3. When ready, the cooker will switch to WARM mode. Press STEAM and let the rice cook for 10 minutes more. Fluff with a spoon, discard garlic and serve hot!

Nutrition Values (Per Serving)

Calories: 391 Fat: 4g Carbohydrates: 69g Protein: 8g

Spicy Cajun Crawfish Tails with Rice

Servings: 4 | Prep Time: 15 minutes | Cooking Time: 45 minutes

Ingredients

1 ½ cups uncooked long-grain rice
1 green bell pepper, diced
1 small onion, diced
1 bunch green onions, diced
1 pound peeled crawfish tails
1 (14 ounce) can chicken broth
1 (10 ounce) can diced tomatoes with green chile pepper
4 tablespoons butter
1 tablespoon dried parsley
1 teaspoon Cajun seasoning

Directions

1. Add rice, onion, green pepper, green onion, crawfish tails, chicken broth, diced tomatoes, parsley, butter, Cajun seasoning in a large bowl.
2. Mix well and pour the mixture into your Aroma Cooker.
3. Close the lid, push the WHITE RICE button, and let the cooking cycle complete. When ready, open the lid and season to taste before serving.

Nutrition Values (Per Serving)

Calories: 462 Fat: 27g Carbohydrates: 55g Protein: 22g

Bacon and Onion Rice

Servings: 3 | Prep Time: 10 minutes | Cooking Time: 20-30 minutes

Ingredients

1 ½ cups uncooked white rice
3 tablespoons butter
4-6 bacon slices
½ medium-sized onion

Directions

1. Cut onion into ½-inch chunks and slice bacon into ¼-inch square pieces.
2. Add the rice to your Aroma cooker and pour water until line 2.
3. Close the lid and cook on WHITE RICE mode until the cooking cycle completes.
4. Take a medium-sized frying pan and place it over medium heat. Add bacon and fry it until crisp, it should take around 2-3 minutes.
5. Once the rice is ready, carefully open the lid and stir in butter. Add the bacon onion mixture and give it a good stir. Serve hot and enjoy.

Nutrition Values (Per Serving)

Calories: 499 Fat: 23g Carbohydrates: 55g Protein: 16g

Creamy Chicken Mushroom Rice

Servings: 4 | Prep Time: 5 minutes | Cooking Time: 45-55 minutes

Ingredients

2 chicken brests, halved, julienned
4 cups uncooked white rice, rinsed well
2 cups chicken broth
½ cup dried shiitake mushrooms
½ cup frozen peas, unthawed
½ cup table cream
1 teaspoon fish sauce
Dash black pepper
Dash kosher salt
Water
¼ cup fresh cilantro, minced for garnish

Directions

1. Add dried mushrooms in a bowl and soak them in 2 cups of water for 1 hour.
2. Remove and discard the stem. Mince the cap. Reserve 1 cup of the soaking liquid.
3. Lay the chicken fillets in steamer tray and season with salt and pepper.
4. Place all the ingredients to your Aroma Cooker except for the chicken and cream.
5. Add water to 4 level mark. Place steam tray on top.
6. Close the lid, press WHITE RICE button, and let the cooking cycle complete.
7. When done, remove the lid and take the steamer tray out.
8. Fold in cream into the rice and stir. Add the steamed chicken to the rice and stir.
9. Sprinkle with freshly minced cilantro and serve immediately.

Nutrition Values (Per Serving)

Calories: 165 Fat: 4g Carbohydrates: 15g Protein: 16g

Chicken and Ginger Rice Meal

Servings: 4 | Prep Time: 10 minutes | Cooking Time: 20-30 minutes

Ingredients

1 cup coconut milk, unsweetened
3 cups baby spinach, packed
1 piece 2-inch long sliced ginger, peeled
1 ¼ pounds chicken breasts, cubed and boneless
1 cup jasmine rice, washed
¾ cup water
1 large bouillon cube, chicken
Salt to taste

Directions

1. Take a bowl full of hot water and dissolve bouillon cube.
2. Add chicken, ginger and rice to your Aroma Cooker.
3. Arrange spinach on top.
4. Pour broth and coconut milk and give it a good stir.
5. Season with salt and close the lid.
6. Push the WHITE RICE button and wait for the cooking cycle to complete.
7. When ready, the cooker will switch to WARM mode. Let the mixture stand for 5 minutes. Open the lid, and fluff the rice.
8. Serve immediately.

Nutrition Values (Per Serving)

Calories: 296 Fat: 6g Carbohydrates: 24g Protein: 34g

Mouthwatering Curry Chicken Jambalaya

Servings: 4 | Prep Time: 10 minutes | Cooking Time: 35-40 minutes

Ingredients

2 tablespoons oil
1 cup onion, chopped
1 tablespoon garlic, minced
2 tablespoons curry powder
2 cups water
1 can tomato sauce (8 ounce)
1 pack jambalaya mix (8 ounce)
1 pound boneless and skinless chicken breast, cut into 1-inch cubes
½ cup golden raisins
¾ cup plain yogurt
⅓ cup chopped cashews

Directions

1. Heat oil in the Aroma Rice Cooker on WHITE RICE mode.
2. Stir in the garlic and sauté for 1 minute.
3. Add curry powder and sauté for another minute.
4. Pour in the water, tomato sauce, Jambalaya mix and raisins.
5. Close the lid, push the WHITE RICE button.
6. Let the cooking cycle complete.
7. Once the cooker switches to WARM mode, open the lid and stir in yogurt.
8. Let it simmer for about 5 minutes.
9. Serve sprinkled with cashews.

Nutrition Values (Per Serving)

Calories: 562 Fat: 17g Carbohydrates: 72g Protein: 37g

Dill And Lemon "Feta" Rice

Servings: 3 | Prep Time: 5 minutes | Cooking Time: 45 minutes

Ingredients

- 1 ½ cups long-grain white rice
- 2 cups chicken stock
- 2 tablespoons olive oil
- 2 small boiling onions, finely chopped
- ¼ cup pine nuts
- ¼ cup fresh lemon juice
- 1 tablespoon fresh dill, minced
- 1 ½ teaspoons fresh mint, minced
- 1 cup crumbled feta
- 1 lemon, cut in 8 wedges

Directions

1. Grease your Aroma Cooker's inner pot with cooking spray. Add the rice and stock.
2. Close the lid, push the WHITE RICE button, and let the cooking cycle complete.
3. Once the cooker switches to WARM, let the rice simmer for 10 minutes.
4. When ready, carefully open the lid.
5. Heat oil in a skillet over medium heat. Stir in onions and cook for 5 minutes.
6. Add in pine nuts and cook until golden; this should take about a minute.
7. Transfer the onions and pine nuts to the rice cooker.
8. Sprinkle with lemon juice, dill and mint, and stir gently.
9. Cover and keep in WARM mode for 10 more minutes. Next, transfer to a serving dish and top with feta and lemon wedges.

Nutrition Values (Per Serving)

Calories: 254 Fat: 6g Carbohydrates: 45g Protein: 5g

Simple Salmon and Rice Delight

Servings: 6 | Prep Time: 10 minutes | Cooking Time: 40-45 minutes

Ingredients

2 salmon fillets
2 teaspoons ground ginger
3 tablespoons soy sauce
1 garlic clove, minced
2 teaspoons brown sugar
½ teaspoon red pepper flakes
1 green onion, sliced
2 cups brown rice
Salt and black pepper to taste

Directions

1. In a bowl, mix ginger, soy sauce, brown sugar, and chili flakes. Place the fish into the marinade and refrigerate for 30 minutes.
2. Add 2 cups of brown rice to your Aroma cooker and pour water until line 2.
3. Close the lid, push the WHITE RICE button, and let the cooking cycle complete.
4. In the meantime, take the fish out of the fridge and place it on a steamer basket.
5. After 30 minutes of cooking, carefully open the lid and add the steamer basket with the salmon fillets.
6. Close the lid and let the cooking cycle complete.
7. Once the cycle is over, open the lid and check if the salmon flakes easily with a fork. If not, close and let it cook for a few minutes more.
8. Serve the rice over the salmon and sprinkle with freshly sliced green onion.

Nutrition Values (Per Serving)

Calories: 460 Fat: 28g Carbohydrates: 77g Protein: 37g

Traditional Basmati Rice

Servings: 6 | Prep Time: 5 minutes | Cooking Time: 30-35 minutes

Ingredients

2 cups Basmati rice, rinsed and drained
Water, to fill up to line 2
Salt to taste
Fresh parsley, chopped

Directions

1. Add the rice to your Aroma Cooker. Fill the inner pot with water up to line 2.
2. Stir and close the lid. Press WHITE RICE and let the cooking cycle complete.
3. Once the cooker switches to WARM mode, open the lid and allow it to sit for 10 min. Fluff the rice and garnish with parsley before serving.

Nutrition Values (Per Serving)

Calories: 234 Fat: 0g Carbohydrates: 47g Protein: 4g

Southwestern Rice Cooker Quinoa Yum

Servings: 5 | Prep Time: 10 minutes | Cooking Time: 50-60 minutes

Ingredients

12 ounce boxed quinoa
1 can of 10 ounce undrained tomatoes and green chili peppers
1 can of 15-oz black beans, rinsed and drained
½ a small pack taco seasoning, dry

Directions

1. Take a bowl and mix in taco seasoning, quinoa, 1 cup of water, tomatoes, pepper and beans. Transfer the mixture to your Aroma cooker.
2. Close the lid, push the BROWN RICE button, and let the cooking cycle complete. When ready, open the lid, fluff the rice and serve immediately.

Nutrition Values (Per Serving)

Calories: 512 Fat: 31g Carbohydrates: 88g Protein: 32g

Fine Chile Cheese Rice

Servings: 8 | Prep Time: 10 minutes | Cooking Time: 25-35 minutes

Ingredients

- 2 cups white rice
- 3 cups chicken broth
- 1 can (4 ounces) diced green chilies
- ½ medium onion, diced
- 2 teaspoons garlic powder
- 1 cup Monterey Jack Cheese, shredded
- 1 tablespoon butter

Directions

1. Take a skillet and place it over medium heat.
2. Heat the butter, add in onion and garlic.
3. Sauté until translucent, for 1-2 minutes.
4. Then transfer to your Aroma cooker, along with rice, chilies and broth.
5. Give it a good stir and close the lid.
6. Cook on WHITE RICE mode until the cooking cycle is over.
7. Once cooked, open the lid and sprinkle with the shredded cheese.
8. Let it sit in WARM mode with the lid closed for 5-7 minutes to melt the cheese. Next, carefully open the lid, stir gently and serve immediately.

Nutrition Values (Per Serving)

Calories: 291 Fat: 9g Carbohydrates: 42g Protein: 11g

Peanut Butter Rice

Servings: 4 | Prep Time: 10 minutes | Cooking Time: 20-30 minutes

Ingredients

- 3 bell peppers, finely chopped
- 1 cup soaked white rice
- ¼ cup peanut butter
- ¼ cup tomato puree
- 1 teaspoon paprika powder
- 1 teaspoon salt
- 2 cups water

Directions

1. In a bowl, mix in water and peanut butter, then set aside for 10 minutes.
2. Add the rest of the ingredients to your Aroma Cooker. Give it a good stir and add in the peanut butter mix.
3. Close the lid, push the WHITE RICE button, and let the cooking cycle complete. When done, carefully open the lid, stir and serve warm.

Nutrition Values (Per Serving)

Calories: 107 Fat: 8g Carbohydrates: 6g Protein: 1g

Original Moroccan Brown Rice

Servings: 5 | Prep Time: 5 minutes| Cooking Time: 45-50 minutes

Ingredients

1 ½ cups long-grain brown rice
2 ¾ cups water
Salt and pepper to taste
1 teaspoon coriander, ground
½ teaspoon cardamom, ground
3 tablespoons butter, cut in pieces
¼ cup preserved lemon, minced for garnish

Directions

1. Grease the Aroma cooker with cooking spray. Add rice, water, coriander and cardamom. Season with salt and pepper, and stir gently.
2. Close the lid, press BROWN RICE, and let the cooking cycle complete.
3. When ready, carefully open the lid and stir in butter.
4. Close the lid and let it sit in WARM mode for 10 minutes.
5. After 10 minutes, open the lid, fluff the rice and squeeze lemon. Serve warm.

Nutrition Values (Per Serving)

Calories: 423 Fat: 33g Carbohydrates: 41g Protein: 29g

Rice and Chinese Sausage

Servings: 6 | Prep Time: 5 minutes | Cooking Time: 1 hour

Ingredients

2 cups medium-grain white rice
1 cup Chinese sausage, thinly sliced diagonally
½ cup green onions, thinly sliced
2 ¾ cups water
¼ cup cilantro leaf, garnish
2 tablespoons black sesame seeds, to garnish

Directions

1. Add rice, water, onions and sausage to your Aroma cooker and stir.
2. Close the lid, push the WHITE RICE button, and let the cooking cycle complete.
3. Once the cooking cycle is over, the cooker will switch to WARM mode.
4. Press STEAM and set timer to 15 minutes.
5. When done, carefully open the lid and fluff the rice.
6. Transfer to a serving dish and garnish with sesame seeds and cilantro.
7. Serve and enjoy.

Nutrition Values (Per Serving)

Calories: 196 Fat: 2g Carbohydrates: 39g Protein: 4g

Almonds Corn Quinoa

Servings: 4 | Prep Time: 10 minutes | Cooking Time: 40-50 minutes

Ingredients

1 cup quinoa
1 carrot, diced
½ cup sweet corn
8-9 almonds
7-8 kale leaves, chopped
1 teaspoon salt
2 cups water
1 teaspoon paprika powder

Directions

1. Place the quinoa in your Rice Cooker. Add the rest of the ingredients and stir gently.
2. Close the lid, press BROWN RICE button, and let the cooking cycle complete.
3. Once the cooker switches to WARM mode, let it rest for 5 minutes.
4. Serve with sliced avocado and tempeh (optionally).

Nutrition Values (Per Serving)

Calories: 181 Fat: 5g Carbohydrates: 1g Protein: 7g

Cashew And Cherry Rice

Servings: 4 | Prep Time: 10 minutes | Cooking Time: 20-30 minutes

Ingredients

½ cup long-grain white rice
½ cup fresh cherries, chopped
¼ cup cashew paste
½ teaspoon salt
¼ teaspoon cinnamon powder
½ cup almond milk
½ cup water

Directions

1. Add all of the ingredients to your Aroma Cooker. Stir gently.
2. Close the lid, press WHITE RICE button, and let the cooking cycle complete.
3. Once the cooker switches to WARM mode, let it simmer for 7-10 minutes.
4. Open the lid, stir and serve warm.

Nutrition Values (Per Serving)

Calories: 453 Fat: 26g Carbohydrates: 88g Protein: 21g

Mesmerizing Garlic And Chicken Fragrant Rice

Servings: 3 | Prep Time: 10 minutes | Cooking Time: 35-40 minutes

Ingredients

- 3 cups uncooked jasmine rice
- 3 cups water
- 2 tablespoons sesame oil
- 2 cubs chicken bouillon
- ½ cup olive oil
- 1 green onion, chopped
- 2 cloves garlic, smashed
- 1 2-inch piece fresh ginger root, crushed
- 1 chicken thigh with skin

Directions

1. Add rice, water, chicken bouillon, sesame oil, green onion, garlic and ginger to your Aroma Cooker. Swirl gently. Place the chicken on thigh on top.
2. Close the lid, press WHITE RICE button, and let the cooking cycle complete.
3. When done, carefully open the lid and serve immediately.

Nutrition Values (Per Serving)

Calories: 423 Fat: 23g Carbohydrates: 15g Protein: 31g

Simplest Tomato Rice

Servings: 5 | Prep Time: 10 minutes | Cooking Time: 45 minutes

Ingredients

- 2 teaspoons olive oil
- 1 tomato, large, stems removed, chopped
- 2 cups white rice, washed
- ⅔ teaspoon salt
- ¼ teaspoon ground black pepper

Directions

1. Add rice to your Aroma Cooker and pour water until level 2.
2. Stir and remove 5-6 tablespoons of water from the cooker.
3. Add in olive oil, stir in the tomato and season with salt and pepper.
4. Close the lid, push WHITE RICE, and let the cooking cycle complete.
5. Once ready, carefully open the lid and fluff the rice.
6. Serve and enjoy!

Nutrition Values (Per Serving)

Calories: 322 Fat: 10g Carbohydrates: 54g Protein: 6g

Sweet Ginger Porridge

Servings: 4 | Prep Time: 5 minutes | Cooking Time: 20-30 minutes

Ingredients

4 tablespoons honey
5 cups filtered water
1 cup rice, short grain, washed
1 tablespoon ginger, freshly grated
1 teaspoon kosher salt

Directions

1. Wash the rice thoroughly and add it to your Aroma Cooker. Season with salt and ginger. Stir well and close the lid.
2. Cook on STEAM mode for 20-25 minutes until the desired consistency is obtained.
3. Once ready, carefully open the lid and stir well.
4. Divide among rice bowls and serve with a drizzle of honey.

Nutrition Values (Per Serving)

Calories: 205 Fat: 3g Carbohydrates: 44g Protein: 4g

Toasted Coconut Yellow Rice

Servings: 4 | Prep Time: 10 minutes | Cooking Time: 25-35 minutes

Ingredients

- 2 cups white rice, rinsed
- 1 can (14 ounce) coconut milk
- 1 ¼ cups water
- ¼ cup sweetened flaked coconut
- 1 teaspoon ground turmeric
- ½ teaspoon kosher salt

Directions

1. Place the rice in the Aroma cooker.
2. Heat coconut milk, water, half flaked coconut, turmeric and salt in a small pan over medium heat.
3. Cook for 7-10 minutes until the turmeric dissolves and the color is uniform.
4. Transfer the mixture over to the rice cooker.
5. Close the lid, push the WHITE RICE button, and let the cooking cycle complete.
6. In the meantime, toast the remaining coconut flakes for 5 minutes in a skillet over medium heat.
7. Once the cooker switches to WARM mode, let it sit for 5 minutes.
8. Then, carefully open the lid and fluff the rice.
9. Sprinkle with the toasted coconut and serve.

Nutrition Values (Per Serving)

Calories: 382 Fat: 24g Carbohydrates: 56g Protein: 22g

Authentic Thai Chicken Rice

Servings: 4 | Prep Time: 10 minutes | Cooking Time: 35-45 minutes

Ingredients

1 red pepper, sliced
3 cups rice, washed and uncooked
2 chicken breasts, cubed

For Sauce

1 can chunked pineapple with ¼ cup juice
1 can milk, coconut
½ teaspoon ginger, powdered
1 tablespoon ginger, grated
1 teaspoon five spice powder, Chinese

Directions

1. Add the rice to your Aroma cooker and pour water up to line 3.
2. Close the lid, push the WHITE RICE button, and let the cooking cycle complete.
3. In the meantime, heat 1 tablespoon of oil in a small pan over medium heat.
4. Add in the chicken cubes and cook them for 4-5 minutes or until slightly undercooked.
5. Once chicken is nearly cooked, lower down the heat to low.
6. Take a bowl and whisk in all the sauce ingredients.
7. Pour the sauce over the chicken and cook for 8-10 minutes.
8. Once the Aroma cooker completes the cycle and switches to WARM mode, transfer the rice to a serving platter.
9. Serve a portion the rice with the sauce and the chicken on top.

Nutrition Values (Per Serving)

Calories: 489 Fat: 32g Carbohydrates: 79g Protein: 36g

Rocking And Flying Risotto

Servings: 4 | Prep Time: 10 minutes | Cooking Time: 40-45 minutes

Ingredients

- 2 tablespoons olive oil
- 16 ounces mushrooms, sliced
- 3 tablespoons butter
- 2 cups Arborio rice
- 1 shallot, diced
- 1 clove garlic, minced
- ½ cup white wine
- 4 ½ cups chicken broth
- 1 teaspoon salt
- ½ teaspoon black pepper
- ⅓ cup grated parmesan
- ⅔ cup peas
- 1 tablespoon butter

Directions

1. Heat oil in a skillet over medium heat. Add the mushrooms and shallots and cook for 5-7 minutes or until tender. Then, remove from heat and set aside.
2. Push the STEAM button of your Aroma Rice Cooker and set the timer to 35 minutes.
3. Melt butter and add in the rice. Stir in garlic, wine, 2 cups of stock, salt and pepper.
4. Close the lid and cook for 10 minutes.
5. Once ready, open the lid and stir in the mushrooms and rest of the stock.
6. Cook for 17 more minutes. Stir in peas and 1 tablespoon of butter.
7. Sprinkle with freshly grated parmesan cheese and serve immediately.

Nutrition Values (Per Serving)

Calories: 247 Fat: 7g Carbohydrates: 32g Protein: 12g

Hearty Bacon Rice

Servings: 4 | Prep Time: 10 minutes | Cooking Time: 30 minutes

Ingredients

2 cups white rice
2 cups beef stock
1 tablespoon oil
8 ounces bacon, cut in strips
1 onion, sliced
1 teaspoon garlic, minced
1 cup frozen mixed vegetables
2 tablespoons soy sauce

Directions

1. Push the STEAM button and set timer to 10 minutes.
2. Heat oil and stir in the bacon and onion.
3. Sauté for 4-5 minutes or until the onion is translucent.
4. Add in the garlic and cook for another minute.
5. Next, add the rice and stir to coat well.
6. Add the vegetables, beef stock and stir gently.
7. Close the lid, push the WHITE RICE button, and let the cooking cycle complete.
8. When ready, carefully open the lid and stir in soy sauce.
9. Serve immediately and enjoy.

Nutrition Values (Per Serving)

Calories: 525 Fat: 28g Carbohydrates: 70g Protein: 29g

"Pirates Of The Caribbean" Rice

Servings: 4 | Prep Time: 5 minutes | Cooking Time: 30-40 minutes

Ingredients

1 cup white rice, rinsed
1 teaspoon ground Jamaican jerk spiced
1 sprig thyme, stem discarded
1 garlic clove, minced
1 teaspoon ginger, grated
2 scallions, sliced
¾ cup sweet potatoes, finely diced
⅓ cup toasted coconut flakes
⅓ cup raisins
⅓ cup red pepper, diced
1 cup vegetable broth

Directions

1. Add all the listed ingredients to your Aroma Cooker, except for the scallions and coconut flakes.
2. Pour broth and close the lid. Press WHITE RICE and let the cooking cycle complete. When ready, carefully open the lid and fluff the rice with a fork.
3. Transfer to a serving dish and garnish with coconut and scallions.

Nutrition Values (Per Serving)

Calories: 278 Fat: 24g Carbohydrates: 15g Protein: 4g

Spicy Cajun Wild Rice

Servings: 6 | Prep Time: 10 minutes | Cooking Time: 55-65 minutes

Ingredients

1 cup uncooked wild rice
1 can chicken broth (14 ounce)
¼ cup water
½ pound Andouille sausage, diced

½ cup diced sweet onion
1 cup chopped fresh mushrooms
1 tablespoon garlic, minced

1 can (10 ounce) condensed cream mushroom soup

Directions

1. Add wild rice, chicken broth, sausage, water, mushrooms and garlic to your Aroma Cooker. Press the STEAM button and set timer to 40 minutes.
2. Wait until the mixture starts to boil, with the lid open, and stir gently.
3. Close the lid and let it cook for the remaining cycle or until the rice is tender.
4. When ready, open the lid and stir in the ream mushroom soup. Serve hot.

Nutrition Values (Per Serving)

Calories: 297 Fat: 15g Carbohydrates: 26g Protein: 16g

Peanut Rice and Bell Pepper

Servings: 6 | Prep Time: 5 minutes | Cooking Time: 25 minutes

Ingredients

3 bell peppers, finely chopped
1 cup soaked white rice
1 red onion, finely chopped
¼ cup peanut butter

¼ cup tomato puree
1 teaspoon paprika powder
1 teaspoon sea salt
2 cups water

Directions

1. Take a bowl and mix in peanut butter and ¼ cup of water, then set aside.
2. Stir in all the other ingredients to your Aroma Cooker.
3. Pour the peanut butter mix in the cooker. Close the lid, push the WHITE RICE button, and let the cooking cycle complete.
4. Once the pot switches to WARM mode, remove the lid and stir. Serve warm.

Nutrition Values (Per Serving)

Calories: 368 Fat: 9g Carbohydrates: 63g Protein: 10g

Exciting Shrimp and Quail Eggs With Java Rice

Servings: 4 | Prep Time: 5 minutes | Cooking Time: 40 minutes

Ingredients

- 12 whole quail eggs, raw
- ¼ cup fresh leeks, minced, for garnish

For Rice

- 2 cups mushrooms
- 2 cups uncooked white rice, rinsed
- 1 cup frozen peas, thawed
- 1 cup frozen shrimps, unthawed
- ¼ teaspoon fish sauce
- 1 pinch of black pepper and salt
- Water
- 2 tablespoons butter
- Ice bath (2 parts water + 1 parts ice cube)

Garnish

- ¼ cup fresh parsley, minced
- 1 teaspoon toasted garlic cloves

Directions

1. Add quail eggs in a steam tray.
2. Add all the ingredients, except the eggs and butter, to your Aroma Cooker. Pour water until line 4 and place the steam tray on top.
3. Close the lid, push the WHITE RICE button, let the cooking cycle complete.
4. Once the Aroma Cooker switches to WARM mode, open the lid.
5. Transfer the steamed eggs to an ice bath and soak them.
6. Pat them dry with paper towels and peel the skin, cut them in halves lengthwise.
7. Fold in butter in your rice and season to taste.
8. Serve with eggs on top and garnish with leeks (optional).

Nutrition Values (Per Serving)
Calories: 497 Fat: 23g Carbohydrates: 59g Protein: 36g

Shiitake Black Bean Rice

Servings: 6 | Prep Time: 5 minutes | Cooking Time: 25-35 minutes

Ingredients

- 1 cup shiitake button mushroom, diced
- 1 cup long-grain rice
- ½ cup cooked black beans
- 1 red onion, finely chopped
- 3 garlic cloves, minced
- 1 ½ teaspoons olive oil
- 2 tablespoons onion powder
- 2 cups water
- ¾ tablespoon sea salt

Directions

1. Push the STEAM button and set timer to 5 minutes.
2. Heat the olive oil and stir in the onions.
3. Sauté for 2 minutes until translucent.
4. Add in the garlic and cook for 1 minute until fragrant.
5. Then, add in the remaining ingredients and close the lid.
6. Push the WHITE RICE button and let the cooking cycle complete.
7. Once ready, carefully open the lid and stir well before serving.

Nutrition Values (Per Serving)
Calories: 304 Fat: 17g Carbohydrates: 33g Protein: 13g

Dirty Rice And Chinese Chorizo

Servings: 4 | Prep Time: 5 minutes | Cooking Time: 40 minutes

Ingredients

A handful asparagus, thick-stemmed with tough ends snapped f, sliced in halves
Olive for drizzle
Sea salt to taste

For Rice

2 pieces, medium Chinese Chorizo, diced
2 cups mushrooms broth
2 cups white long-grain rice
1 cup frozen peas, thawed
1 can of 15-oz button mushrooms, pieces and stems rinsed and drained
1 teaspoon garlic powder
1 pinch of black pepper
1 pinch of kosher salt
Water
Freshly chopped parsley

Garnish

¼ cup fresh parsley, minced
1 teaspoon toasted garlic cloves

Directions

1. Place asparagus in a steam tray and season with salt. Drizzle olive oil on top.
2. Stir in all the ingredients into the rice cooker.
3. Add water up to line 4 and place the steam tray on top.
4. Close the lid, press WHITE RICE button, and let the cooking cycle complete.
5. Once it goes off, carefully open the lid and remove the steam tray.
6. Drain the asparagus.

7. Serve by ladling 1 portion of rice into a plate.
8. Sprinkle with freshly chopped parsley.
9. Garnish with a portion of asparagus and enjoy.

Nutrition Values (Per Serving)

Calories: 498 Fat: 24g Carbohydrates: 54g Protein: 26g

Jasmine Rice Pilaf

Servings: 8 | Prep Time: 5 minutes | Cooking Time: 35 minutes

Ingredients

2 cups jasmine rice, rinsed and drained
Chicken stock to fill up to line 2
¼ cup almonds, chopped
½ cup button mushrooms, halved
1 shallot, minced
½ tablespoon butter
1 garlic clove, minced

Directions

1. Add the rice to your Aroma Rice Cooker.
2. Melt butter in a small pan over medium heat. Stir in shallots and cook for 2 minutes. Add in mushrooms and cook for 1 minute more, then remove from heat.
3. Transfer the sautéed ingredients and the chopped almonds into the rice cooker. Fill the inner pot with broth up to line 2. Stir and close the lid.
4. Press the WHITE RICE button and let the cooking cycle complete.
5. Once the cooker switches to WARM mode, let the rice sit for 10 minutes.
6. Fluff the rice and transfer to serving bowls.

Nutrition Values (Per Serving)

Calories: 198 Fat: 3g Carbohydrates: 38g Protein: 3g

Healthy Mexican Green Rice

Servings: 4 | Prep Time: 10 minutes | Cooking Time: 30 minutes

Ingredients

1 tablespoon unsalted butter
½ small white onion, chopped
1 cup long-grain white rice
1 ½ cups water
½ teaspoon salt
½ cup fresh cilantro leaves, minced

Directions

1. Push the STEAM button and set timer to 5 minutes.
2. Melt the butter and stir in the onions. Sauté for 2-3 minutes until translucent.
3. Add in rice, salt, water, cilantro and give it a good stir.
4. Close the lid, press BROWN RICE button, and let the cooking cycle complete.
5. Once the cooker switches to WARM mode, press the STEAM button and let the rice STEAM for 15 minutes.
6. Once ready, fluff the rice and serve.

Nutrition Values (Per Serving)

Calories: 129 Fat: 7g Carbohydrates: 13g Protein: 5g

Curious Red Rice

Servings: 8 | Prep Time: 5 minutes | Cooking Time: 65 minutes

Ingredients

2 cups red rice, rinsed and drained
Water to fill up to line 2
Butter for grease
Salt to taste

Directions

1. Grease the inner cooking pot with butter.
2. Add rice to your Rice Cooker and season with salt.
3. Fill the cooker with water up to line 2 mark. Swirl and close the lid.
4. Press the BROWN RICE button and let the cooking cycle complete.
5. Once the Aroma Cooker switches to WARM mode, let the rice sit for 10 minutes.
6. Then, fluff the rice and transfer to serving bowls.

Nutrition Values (Per Serving)

Calories: 226 Fat: 3g Carbohydrates: 43g Protein: 6g

Coconut Rice and Roasted Almonds

Servings: 6 | Prep Time: 5 minutes | Cooking Time: 25-35 minutes

Ingredients

1 cup white rice
2 cups coconut milk
¼ cup shaved coconut

8-9 almonds
½ teaspoon cardamom powder
½ teaspoon sea salt

Directions

1. Add all the listed ingredients to your Aroma Cooker, except for the almonds.
2. Close the lid, press WHITE RICE button, and let the cooking cycle complete.
3. Once the cooker switches to WARM mode, let it sit for 10 minutes.
4. In the meantime, toast the almonds in a skillet over medium heat.
5. Open the lid and add in the toasted almonds.
6. Give it a good stir and serve.

Nutrition Values (Per Serving)

Calories: 323 Fat: 7g Carbohydrates: 69g Protein: 10g

Chicken Biryani And Saffron Cream

Servings: 4 | Prep Time: 5 minutes | Cooking Time: 40 minutes

Ingredients

- 1 pound chicken breast
- 1 cup plain yogurt
- 1 ½ teaspoons coriander
- 1 teaspoon turmeric
- ½ teaspoon cumin
- 1 onion, diced
- 1 piece 2-inch fresh ginger, peeled
- 3 garlic cloves, peeled
- 1 jalapeno, stemmed
- 3 tablespoons canola oil
- 1 ½ cups white rice
- 6 cloves garlic
- 1 cinnamon stick
- 3 cups chicken broth
- 1 teaspoon salt
- 1 pinch of saffron mixed with 2 tablespoons of heavy cream
- 3 tablespoons cilantro, chopped
- 3 tablespoons mint, chopped
- 1 lime

Directions

1. Cut the chicken breast into chunks. Take a bowl and add yogurt and powdered spices, then add the chicken and coat it well. Set aside.
2. In a food processor, puree onion, ginger, garlic and chili pepper. Set aside.
3. Push the STEAM button and set timer to 20 minutes. Pour the oil and heat it.
4. Add in the onion paste and cook until the liquid starts to evaporate and the paste is slightly brown; this should take about 15 minutes.

5. Next, add the rice, whole spices and give it a good stir. Smooth the top and place the marinated chicken pieces on top.
6. Pour broth and season with salt. Close the lid, push the WHITE RICE button, and let the cooking cycle complete.
7. Once the cooker switches to WARM, open the lid and stir in saffron cream and mix.
8. Sprinkle with chopped cilantro and mint. Close the lid again, push the STEAM button and set timer to 5 minutes. Once ready, carefully open the lid, squeeze lime and fluff the rice.
9. Scoop onto a serving platter and garnish with freshly chopped cilantro, cashews, fried onion or raisins.

Nutrition Values (Per Serving)

Calories: 585 Fat: 18g Carbohydrates: 3g Protein: 33g

Fuss Free Simple Risotto

Servings: 2-4 | Prep Time: 5 minutes | Cooking Time: 45 minutes

Ingredients

1 ½ cups Arborio rice
4 ½ cups hot chicken stock
1 cup grated parmesan cheese

Directions

1. Add rice and chicken stock to your Aroma Cooker.
2. Close the lid, press BROWN RICE button, and let the cooking cycle complete.
3. Once it goes off, carefully open the lid and fluff the rice.
4. Close the lid and let it on in WARM mode for 10 minutes.
5. Sprinkle parmesan cheese on top, stir and serve immediately.

Nutrition Values (Per Serving)

Calories: 485 Fat: 18g Carbohydrates: 67g Protein: 12g

Delicious Saffron Yellow Rice With Fruit Chutney

Servings: 6 | Prep Time: 5 minutes | Cooking Time: 35 minutes

Ingredients

- 3 cups basmati rice, rinsed
- 3 cups water
- 1 pinch powdered saffron
- 2 tablespoons fruit chutney
- 2-4 cardamom pods, split and use seeds
- Salt and Pepper, to taste
- 1 ounce butter
- 2-4 sprigs fresh coriander, optional

Directions

1. Place 3 cups Basmati rice in your Aroma Cooker. Pour water up to line 3.
2. Add saffron, cardamom seeds, chutney. Season with salt and pepper.
3. Close the lid, press WHITE RICE button, and let the cooking cycle complete.
4. Once it goes off, carefully open the lid and stir in butter, mix gently to combine. Garnish with freshly chopped coriander and top with toasted flakes.

Nutrition Values (Per Serving)

Calories: 314 Fat: 2g Carbohydrates: 76g Protein: 3g

Sensible Mirin Rice

Servings: 2 | Prep Time: 10 minutes | Cooking Time: 25 minutes

Ingredients

- 2 shiitake mushrooms, dried
- Water to reach level 2 mark
- 2 cups medium-grain white rice
- ¾ ounce carrots, peeled
- ⅓ slice fried tofu, chopped in strips
- 1 ounce chicken, cubed
- 1 tablespoon mirin
- 1 tablespoon soy sauce, light
- ¼ teaspoon dashinomoto
- ⅓ teaspoon kosher salt

Directions

1. Take a bowl and add dashinomoto, mirin, salt, and soy sauce.
2. Soak the tofu in this mix, keep the soup stock for later use. Slice the carrot into strips.
3. Remove hard tips from shiitake mushrooms, slice them into strips.
4. Pour the soup stock to shiitake water and mix.
5. Add the rice to your Aroma Cooker and pour the already prepared stock.
6. Pour water up to line 2 and stir in the remaining ingredients.
7. Close the lid, select WHITE RICE, and let the cooking cycle complete.
8. Once it goes off, carefully open the lid and fluff the rice. Serve and enjoy!

Nutrition Values (Per Serving)

Calories: 459 Fat: 14g Carbohydrates: 50g Protein: 30

Simplest Curry Rice Ever

Servings: 5 | Prep Time: 5 minutes | Cooking Time: 20 minutes

Ingredients

2 cups uncooked white rice, rinsed and drained
3 cups water
3 tablespoons mild curry powder

Directions

1. Stir in rice, curry powder and water to your Aroma Cooker.
2. Close the lid, press WHITE RICE, and let the cooking cycle complete.
3. Once the cooker switches to WARM mode, let it sit for 5 minutes. Fluff the rice and enjoy!

Nutrition Values (Per Serving)

Calories: 225 Fat: 9g Carbohydrates: 29g Protein: 9g

CHAPTER 2
POLTRY, BEEF, SEAFOOD AND PORK

Delicious Pulled Pork BBQ Loafers

Servings: 4 | Prep Time: 5 minutes | Cooking Time: 30 minutes

Ingredients

- 10-12 ounces pork tenderloins
- 1 cup BBQ sauce
- 1 cup chili sauce
- 1 white onion, peeled and chopped
- 4-6 soft, hefty sandwich buns, split and toasted
- 2 ½ cups water

Directions

1. Cover steam tray with 2 sheets of aluminum foil.
2. Place the tenderloins on the tray.
3. Top the pork with BBQ sauce and chili sauce. Scatter onions on top.
4. Pour water into your pot to line 2 and close the lid.
5. Press the STEAM button and set timer to 25-30 minutes.
6. Check the internal temperature using a thermometer, it should read 160° F.
7. Once the meat is tender, take it out and place on a cutting board.
8. Shred using a fork and mix with the remaining sauce.
9. To serve, mount on or between sandwich buns.

Nutrition Values (Per Serving)

Calories: 501 Fat: 32g Carbohydrates: 4g Protein: 46g

Juicy Chicken Paella

Servings: 4 | Prep Time: 10 minutes | Cooking Time: 55 minutes

Ingredients

1 ½ cups basmati rice
4 cups chicken stock
¾ pound skinless and boneless chicken breast
¼ pound shrimps, peeled, deveined and chopped
¼ chopped brown onion
1 cup water
3 ounces green chilies
6 ounces unsalted tomato sauce
1 tomato , diced
1 tablespoon olive oil
¾ teaspoon ground cumin
4 teaspoons chili powder
¼ teaspoon smoked paprika

Directions

1. Coat the rice cooker with olive oil.
2. Add all the ingredients in the order given above.
3. Stir gently, then close the lid.
4. Press the BROWN RICE button and let the cooking cycle complete.
5. When ready, the cooker will switch to WARM mode.
6. Carefully open the lid and serve hot.

Nutrition Values (Per Serving)

Calories: 585 Fat: 33g Carbohydrates: 50g Protein: 32g

Rustic Meatballs Spaghettis

Servings: 4 | Prep Time: 5 minutes | Cooking Time: 30 minutes

Ingredients

- 1 jar marinara sauce
- 3 ½ cups water
- ½ pound spaghetti
- 1 pound meatballs
- 2 large cloves garlic, minced
- 2 tablespoons parsley, chopped
- 1 teaspoon Italian herbs

Directions

1. Take a bowl and add all the listed ingredients. Mix them well and transfer them to your Aroma Cooker.
2. Push the STEAM button and set timer to 20 minutes.
3. Close the lid and let the cooking cycle complete. Once done, open the lid and stir well. Serve and enjoy!

Nutrition Values (Per Serving)

Calories: 476 Fat: 20g Carbohydrates: 63g Protein: 13g

California Turkey And Avocado Salad

Servings: 4 | Prep Time: 5 minutes | Cooking Time: 12 minutes

Ingredients

- 3 large eggs
- 12 ounces turkey cutlets
- 3 ripe avocados, peeled and sliced
- 8 cups assorted salad greens
- ¾ cup blue cheese salad dressing
- 2 cups water
- Salt and pepper to taste

Directions

1. Add water to line 2. Place the unshelled eggs and turkey cutlets in the steamer tray. Season with salt and pepper.
2. Place the tray in your Aroma Cooker and close the lid. Press the STEAM button and set the timer to 12 minutes.
3. Remove the eggs and transfer to a bowl with cold water. Peel and cut them into wedges. Cut the cooked turkey cutlets into matchstick pieces.
4. To assemble, take a salad bowl and add greens, top them with turkey, eggs and sliced avocados. Sprinkle with blue cheese dressing and enjoy.

Nutrition Values (Per Serving)

Calories: 482 Fat: 22g Carbohydrates: 36g Protein: 37g

Holy Shrimp Jambalaya

Servings: 6 | Prep Time: 15 minutes | Cooking Time: 75 minutes

Ingredients

2 cups brown rice
1 pound shrimp, peeled and deveined
1 can (14.5 ounce) chicken broth
1 can (10 ounce) tomato sauce

1 bell pepper, minced
½ cup butter
1 jar mushrooms, undrained

Directions

1. Add the rice, shrimp, chicken broth, bell pepper, tomato sauce, mushrooms and butter to your Aroma Cooker.
2. Close the lid, push the STEAM button, and set timer to 75 minutes.
3. Let the cooking cycle complete but make sure to open the lid every 25 minutes and give it a gentle stir.
4. Once the cooking is over, carefully open the lid and serve immediately!

Nutrition Values (Per Serving)

Calories: 369 Fat: 24g Carbohydrates: 12g Protein: 27g

Beautiful Curried Squash And Pork

Servings: 4 | Prep Time: 20 minutes | Cooking Time: 60 minutes

Ingredients

- 1 tablespoon peanut oil
- 1 lb boneless sirloin pork chop, diced
- 1 ½ tablespoon curry powder
- 2 carrots, sliced
- ½ onion, chopped
- 1 teaspoon fresh garlic, minced
- 14 ounce can chicken broth, undiluted
- 13 ounce low –fat coconut milk
- ¼ cup water
- 1 19 ounce can chickpeas, drained and rinsed
- ¾ cup uncooked brown rice
- 1 cup raw acorn squash, diced

Directions

1. Push the STEAM button and set timer to 15 minutes.
2. Add the oil heat it. Then add the meat and close the lid.
3. Make sure to open the lid every 5 minutes to turn the meat.
4. Next, add the vegetables and cook for 5 minutes more.
5. Cancel the STEAM function and add all the remaining ingredients.
6. Give it a good stir and close the lid.
7. Push BROWN RICE and let cooking cycle complete.
8. Once it goes off, the cooker will switch to WARM mode.
9. Carefully open the lid and serve immediately.

Nutrition Values (Per Serving)

Calories: 256 Fat: 9g Carbohydrates: 19g Protein: 26g

Efficient Paprika Chicken

Servings: 6 | Prep Time: 15 minutes | Cooking Time: 55 minutes

Ingredients

- 3 tablespoons all-purpose flour
- 2 pounds chicken breast, cut into ½ inch strips
- 2 cups chopped onion
- 1 ¼ cups chicken broth
- 2 tablespoons sweet paprika
- 2 teaspoons minced garlic
- 1 teaspoon salt
- 1 pack pre-sliced mushrooms (8 ounce)
- 1 ¼ cups sour cream
- 2 tablespoons olive oil

Directions

1. Push the STEAM button and set timer to 60 minutes. Add the oil and heat it.
2. Stir in onions and cook them for 3 minutes or until translucent.
3. Meanwhile, take a bowl and add flour and chicken. Toss well.
4. Add the chicken to the cooker and cook until brown, for about 4-5 minutes.
5. Add the next 6 ingredients, except for the sour cream and close the lid.
6. Let the STEAM cook cycle complete and wait until it switches to WARM mode. Carefully open the lid and add the sour cream.
7. Give it a good stir and let it heat for a few minutes.
8. Serve hot.

Nutrition Values (Per Serving)

Calories: 265 Fat: 11g Carbohydrates: 11g Protein: 27g

Dijon Chicken Mushroom Platter

Servings: 4 | Prep Time: 5 minutes | Cooking Time: 30 minutes

Ingredients

- ¼ cup parsley, minced
- 1 ½ cups vegetable broth
- 1 cup farro
- 8 ounces crimini mushroom, quartered
- 2 shallots, minced
- 1 teaspoon olive oil
- 4 pieces of 5 ounces chicken breast, skinless and boneless
- 2 cups chicken broth

For Marinade

- 1 tablespoon mustard, Dijon
- 1 teaspoon olive oil
- ⅓ cup balsamic vinegar
- Salt and pepper to taste

Directions

1. Make the marinade by mixing all the ingredients listed under marinade in a zip bag. Add the chicken and coat it well. Refrigerate it for 2 hours.
2. Wait for 2 hours and then press the STEAM button on your rice cooker.
3. Set the timer to 90 minutes. Add oil and heat it. Stir in the shallots and close the lid.
4. Cook for 5 minutes until the shallots become tender. Carefully open the lid and add in the mushrooms. Cook for 8 more minutes, lid closed.
5. Once ready, open the lid, stir in the faro and cook for 3 minutes.
6. Add broth to line 2 and stir. Take the chicken out of the bag and place it inside the cooker. Discard the marinade.
7. Close the lid and let the STEAM cycle to complete.
8. Once it goes off, carefully open the lid.

9. To serve, place the mushroom and faro mix on a plate, and top with the chicken. Sprinkle with parsley and enjoy.

Nutrition Values (Per Serving)

Calories: 301 Fat: 26g Carbohydrates: 2g Protein: 14g

Meatballs From Sweden

Servings: 4 | Prep Time: 5 minutes | Cooking Time: 30 minutes

Ingredients

- 1 pound ground beef
- 4 cups breadcrumbs
- 2 tablespoons mustard
- 1 whole egg
- 2 teaspoons beef bouillon granules
- 2 cups heavy cream
- 1 white onion, chopped
- Salt and pepper to taste
- 2 tablespoons of oil

Directions

1. Take a bowl and add ground beef, bread crumbs, salt, egg and pepper.
2. Mix well and form 2-inch meatballs. Push the STEAM button and set the timer to 30 minutes. Heat the oil and cook the meatballs until browned, about 7-10 minutes.
3. Remove the seared meatballs from your cooker and set aside.
4. Next, add the mustard, heavy cream, beef bouillon granules to your cooker.
5. Stir well and return the meatballs. Close the lid, press STEAM mode and let the cycle complete.
6. Once it goes off, carefully open the lid and serve immediately.

Nutrition Values (Per Serving)

Calories: 377 Fat: 29g Carbohydrates: 11g Protein: 17g

Classic Balsamic Chicken

Servings: 4 | Prep Time: 10 minutes | Cooking Time: 1 hour 20 minutes

Ingredients

- 4 pieces of 6 ounces skinless and boneless chicken breast
- 8 ounces quartered white mushrooms
- 4 tablespoons chopped parsley
- 2 shallots, minced
- 1 teaspoon olive oil
- 1 ½ cups chicken stock
- ½ cup balsamic vinegar
- 2 tablespoons mustard
- 1 cup farro

Directions

1. Mix balsamic vinegar and mustard in a bowl. Add the chicken and let it marinade for 30 minutes. Discard the marinade.
2. In the meantime, press the STEAM button on your Aroma Rice Cooker and set timer to 80 minutes.
3. Add the oil and heat it.
4. Stir in the shallots and cook for 5 minutes.
5. Add the mushrooms and cook for 6-8 minutes. Then, stir in the faro and cook for another 3-5 minutes.
6. Finally, discard the marinade and place the chicken inside the cooker.
7. Close the lid and cook for 1 hour.
8. Once it goes off, the pot will switch to WARM mode.
9. Carefully open the lid, sprinkle with freshly chopped parsley and serve immediately.

Nutrition Values (Per Serving)

Calories: 421 Fat: 7g Carbohydrates: 60g Protein: 30

Delicious Whole Chicken

Servings: 4-6 | Prep Time: 10 minutes | Cooking Time: 40-50 minutes

Ingredients

    3-pound chicken
    2 small onions, peeled, cut in half
    1 lemon, cut in half
    2 sprigs rosemary
    2 tablespoon butter
    Salt and pepper to taste

Directions

1. Place the onions flat on the bottom of your Aroma cooker.
2. Stuff the lemon halves in the chicken along with the rosemary.
3. Coat chicken generously with butter and season with salt and pepper.
4. Place chicken in your rice cooker on top of the sliced onions.
5. Close the lid, press WHITE RICE, and let the cooking cycle complete.
6. Once it goes off, carefully open the lid.
7. Turn around the chicken and push WHITE RICE again, close the lid and let another cooking cycle to complete.
8. Once ready, take the chicken out and broil under a broiler for about 5 minutes for a crispy finish (only if the chicken is slightly undercooked).
9. Serve immediately and enjoy.

Nutrition Values (Per Serving)

Calories: 399 Fat: 27g Carbohydrates: 13g Protein: 34g

Fish Tacos with Sesame Sauce

Servings: 4 | Prep Time: 5 minutes | Cooking Time: 15 minutes

Ingredients

2 cups chicken broth
1 pound mild, white fish fillets
¾ cup sesame salad dressing
3 cups Asian Cole Slaw salad mix
12 small corn tortillas, warm
Salt and pepper to taste

Directions

1. Pour chicken broth to line 2 and add the fish to the steamer tray. Season with salt and pepper, and place the steamer tray in the Aroma cooker.
2. Close the lid and push the STEAM button. Set the timer to 15 minutes and let the cooking cycle complete.
3. Once completed, remove the fish and cut into bite-sized portions. Toss the fish with ¼ cup your salad dressing.
4. Fill each corn tortilla with fish and Cole Slaw. Drizzle more sauce and serve!

Nutrition Values (Per Serving)

Calories: 320 Fat: 17g Carbohydrates: 10g Protein: 33g

Simple Yet Efficient Chicken Chili

Servings: 4 | Prep Time: 10 minutes | Cooking Time: 40 minutes

Ingredients

14 ounce can kidney beans, drained and rinsed
1 pound ground chicken
1 tablespoon tomato paste
1 can black beans, drained and rinsed
1 tablespoon chili powder
2 teaspoons dried oregano
1 cup tomato sauce
1 tablespoon vegetable oil
Salt and pepper to taste

Directions

1. Press the STEAM button and set timer to 40 minutes.
2. Heat the oil, add the chicken pieces and cook for 7-10 minutes until slightly browned.
3. Stir in the beans, tomato paste, sauce and spices.
4. Close the lid and cook for 30 minutes.
5. Once cooked, carefully open the lid and serve immediately.

Nutrition Values (Per Serving)

Calories: 258 Fat: 9g Carbohydrates: 16g Protein: 28g

Beef and Cabbage Roll

Servings: 2 | Prep Time: 15 minutes | Cooking Time: 15 minutes

Ingredients

10 Napa cabbage leaves, blanched
½ pound beef tenderloins, thinly sliced
3 ounces white mushrooms
Salt and pepper to taste

Directions

1. Place the Napa leaves on a flat surface. Arrange the beef slices on top the leaves, and season with salt and pepper. Top with sliced mushrooms.
2. Roll in the cabbage and enclose the beef inside. Place on a plate that can fit in your steaming basket.
3. Place the steaming basket in your Aroma Cooker. Add water up to line 3.
4. Close the lid, push STEAM, and set timer to 15 minutes. Let the cook cycle complete, then carefully open the lid and serve warm.

Nutrition Values (Per Serving)

Calories: 546 Fat: 30g Carbohydrates: 43g Protein: 26g

Chicken with Vegetables

Servings: 4 | Prep Time: 10 minutes | Cooking Time: 45-50 minutes

Ingredients

10 ounce skinless and boneless chicken breast, cut into ½ inch cubes
1 cup white rice
2 cups vegetable stock
½ cup broccoli, cut into florets
½ cup green beans, cut into ½ inch pieces
1 teaspoon oregano, chopped
1 teaspoon thyme, chopped
2 teaspoons vegetable oil
¼ teaspoon cayenne pepper
Salt and pepper to taste

Directions

1. Press the WHITE RICE button on your Aroma Rice Cooker.
2. Heat the oil and add the chicken.
3. Cook the chicken for 4-5 minutes until slightly browned.
4. Add the rest of the ingredients and stir gently.
5. Close the lid and cook until the cycle completes and the rice is tender.
6. Once ready, carefully open the lid and serve hot.

Nutrition Values (Per Serving)

Calories: 309 Fat: 18g Carbohydrates: 19g Protein: 17g

CHAPTER 3
VEGETABLE AND SIDE DISHES RECIPES

Tofu Vegetable Delight

Servings: 4 | Prep Time: 10 minutes | Cooking Time: 20 minutes

Ingredients

- 6 ounces firm tofu, cut into cubes
- 2 tablespoons oyster sauce
- 1 teaspoon toasted sesame oil
- 1 teaspoon vegetable oil
- 1 teaspoon honey
- 1 tablespoon soy sauce
- 1 garlic clove, minced
- ½ bunch asparagus, trimmed and cut into ½ inch slices
- 1 carrot, peeled into matchsticks

Directions

1. Take a bowl and mix in the seasoning.
2. Add the rest the ingredients and toss well.
3. Transfer the mixture to a heatproof bowl.
4. Place the bowl to your Aroma cooker and pour enough water to surround the bowl.
5. Close the lid, push the STEAM button, and set the timer to 20 minutes.
6. Carefully open the lid and serve hot.

Nutrition Values (Per Serving)

Calories: 279 Fat: 19g Carbohydrates: 14g Protein: 18g

Tuna Tomato Tabouleh

Servings: 4 | Prep Time: 5 minutes | Cooking Time: 22minutes

Ingredients

1 cup bulgur wheat, uncooked
½ pound fresh tuna steak
1 cup small grape tomatoes, halved
1 medium cucumber, peeled and diced
¼ cup Italian dressing
2 cups water
Salt and pepper to taste

Directions

1. Pour water until line 2 in your pressure cooker.
2. Add the bulgur wheat.
3. Season with a pinch of salt and pepper.
4. Close the lid, push the STEAM button, and set the timer to 17 minutes.
5. Place tuna on a steam tray.
6. Once cooking is complete, open the lid and place the steam tray inside.
7. STEAM cook for 5 more minutes.
8. Open the lid and remove the tuna, set aside.
9. Allow the Bulgur to cool.
10. Transfer the cooled bulgur to serving bowls and add tomatoes and cucumber.
11. Sprinkle with Italian seasoning.
12. Slice the tuna steak thinly and place on top of the salad.

Nutrition Values (Per Serving)

Calories: 460 Fat: 26g Carbohydrates: 31g Protein: 28g

Simplest Potato Salad Ever

Servings: 4 | Prep Time: 10 minutes | Cooking Time: 15 minutes

Ingredients

- 1 ½ pound small potatoes
- 1 ½ cups water
- 1 ½ cups mayonnaise
- 1 tablespoon extra virgin olive oil
- 1 ½ tablespoons vinegar
- 1 teaspoon celery seeds
- 2 tablespoons chopped onions
- 2 stalks celery, chopped
- 2 teaspoons prepared mustard
- 1 ½ tablespoons pickled relish
- ½ teaspoon salt
- 4 hardboiled eggs, coarsely chopped

Directions

1. Cut the potatoes into bite-sized pieces and add them to your Aroma Cooker.
2. Add water and close the lid.
3. Press STEAM and cook for 12-15 minutes until the potatoes are cooked (tender).
4. Take the rice cooker pan to the sink and run cold water onto the potatoes and eggs, cool them and drain them.
5. Take a bowl and add the potatoes and the eggs.
6. Add the rest the ingredients and toss well.
7. Refrigerate for a while and serve cold.

Nutrition Values (Per Serving)

Calories: 217 Fat: 15g Carbohydrates: 19g Protein: 2g

Healthy Potato Salad

Servings: 6 | Prep Time: 5 minutes | Cooking Time: 20 minutes

Ingredients

1 pound new potatoes, cut into bite-sized portions
1 pound fresh green beans, trimmed and cut in half
½ medium red onion, chopped
½ cup Kalamata olives, pitted
1 tablespoon Dijon mustard
2 cups water
¼ cup extra virgin olive oil
Salt and Pepper to taste

Directions

1. Pour water until line 2. Add the potatoes and season with salt and pepper.
2. Close the lid, push the STEAM button, and set the timer to 10 minutes.
3. Once it goes off, carefully open the lid and add the green beans. Push the STEAM button and cook for 10 minutes.
4. Serve by placing potatoes and beans in a serving bowl and top with red onion and olives. Take a bowl and whisk mustard and oil, season with salt and pepper. Pour the dressing over the vegetables and serve warm.

Nutrition Values (Per Serving)

Calories: 217 Fat: 15g Carbohydrates: 19g Protein: 2g

Snow Peas with Bell Peppers

Servings: 4 | Prep Time: 5 minutes | Cooking Time: 15 minutes

Ingredients

1 tablespoon olive oil
4 shiitake mushrooms, cut in half
1 red bell pepper, seeded and sliced
1 garlic, minced
3 tablespoons water
8 ounces snow peas
Salt and pepper to taste

Directions

1. Push the STEAM cook and set timer for 15 minutes.
2. Pour oil and heat it. Stir in garlic and cook for 1 minute or until fragrant.
3. Add in the mushrooms and cook for 3 minutes. Then, add the snow peas and add water to line 2. Cook for 3 more minutes.
4. Next, add the bell pepper and mix well. Cook for 5 additional minutes.
5. Season with salt and pepper, and serve.

Nutrition Values (Per Serving)

Calories: 94 Fat: 5g Carbohydrates: 20g Protein: 4g

Hearty Squash Delight

Servings: 2 | Prep Time: 5 minutes | Cooking Time: 20 minutes

Ingredients

1 pound small acorn squash, cut into bite-sized portions
1 tablespoon fresh sage
2 tablespoons butter
2 cups water
Salt and Pepper to taste

Directions

1. Add water to line 2. Spoon Acorn Squash into the steam tray, and sprinkle with sage.
2. Place the steam tray into your Rice Cooker and close the lid.
3. Push the STEAM button, set the timer to 20 minutes, and let the cycle complete.
4. Spoon the cooked squash into serving bowls, add a bit butter, salt and pepper.

Nutrition Values (Per Serving)

Calories: 125 Fat: 7g Carbohydrates: 10g Protein: 6g

Brined Olives And Fresh Tomatoes In Couscous

Servings: 4 | Prep Time: 10 minutes | Cooking Time: 45 minutes

Ingredients

1 small lime, sliced into wedges remove pips for garnish

Salad

2 garlic cloves, minced
1 small lime, juiced (reserve 1 tablespoon for garnish)
1 pound ripe cherry tomatoes, quartered
1 pound unripe cherry tomatoes, quartered
¼ teaspoon agave sugar, crumbled
1 teaspoon olive oil
Salt and pepper to taste

For Couscous

2 cups pearl couscous
½ cup Kalamata olive in brine, drained and pitted, roughly chopped
1 cup mushroom broth
½ cup mint, minced
¼ cup fresh parsley, minced
1 teaspoon fresh thyme, minced
Salt and pepper to taste

Directions

1. Take a bowl and whisk lime juice and sugar together.
2. Add the rest of the salad ingredients to the bowl and pour seasoned lime juice on top Give it a good stir and refrigerate.
3. Next, add in the couscous and olives in your Aroma Cooker. Pour broth to line 4. Close the lid, press BROWN RICE, and let the cycle complete.
4. Once it goes off, the cooker will automatically switch to WARM mode.
5. Open the lid and add the rest of the ingredients. Stir well.

6. Adjust seasoning and serve ladling 1 portion couscous into 1 portion tomato salad. Garnish with fresh parsley and a lemon wedge. Enjoy with a squeeze of fresh juice!

Nutrition Values (Per Serving)

Calories: 368 Fat: 9g Carbohydrates: 63g Protein: 10g

Mesmerizing Romano Cheese Pasta

Servings: 4 | Prep Time: 10 minutes | Cooking Time: 25 minutes

Ingredients

2 cups water
1 cup tomato sauce
¼ cup cooked ground beef
¼ teaspoon salt
1 teaspoon olive oil
¼ teaspoon dried oregano
¼ cup Romano cheese, grated
2 cups uncooked rigatoni pasta

Directions

1. Add all the ingredients to your Aroma Cooker, except for the oregano and the cheese.
2. Stir well and season with salt.
3. Close the lid and, press WHITE RICE, and allow the cycle to complete.
4. Once it goes off, the cooker will automatically switch to WARM mode.
5. Carefully open the lid, sprinkle with the grated Romano cheese and the dried oregano.
6. Let it sit on WARM mode for 2-3 minutes until the cheese melts and serve immediately.

Nutrition Values (Per Serving)

Calories: 333 Fat: 9g Carbohydrates: 51g Protein: 13g

Broccoli And Cauliflower Couscous

Servings: 6 | Prep Time: 10 minutes | Cooking Time: 45-55 minutes

Ingredients

For Steamed Vegetables

1 head, small broccoli, sliced into florets, rinsed and drained
1 head, small cauliflower, sliced into florets, drained
Garlic salt

For Couscous

2 cups pearl couscous
1 piece, small shallot, minced
1 teaspoon olive oil
½ teaspoon kosher salt
¼ teaspoon smoked paprika
1 cup mushroom broth

For garnish

1 teaspoon fresh parsley, minced
1 piece, small lime, sliced into wedges

Directions

1. Add cauliflower and broccoli to your steamer tray.
2. Heat oil in a skillet over medium heat. Add in the couscous and sauté until lightly toasted and coated with oil. Transfer to your Aroma Cooker.
3. Add the rest of the ingredients listed under couscous. Give it a good stir.
4. Pour the broth to line 4, and place the steamer tray on top.
5. Close the lid, push BROWN RICE and let the cycle complete.
6. Once ready, the cooker will automatically switch to WARM.
7. Carefully remove the lid and drain the vegetables.
8. Season with a dash of garlic salt, and serve the couscous with veggies.

Nutrition Values (Per Serving)
Calories: 189 Fat: 5g Carbohydrates: 31g Protein: 6g

Spicy Sprouts Pilaf

Servings: 4 | Prep Time: 10 minutes | Cooking Time: 30 minutes

Ingredients

- 1 cup soaked basmati rice
- 1 cup bean sprouts
- 1 tablespoon ginger-garlic paste
- 1 onion, finely chopped
- 2 small red chilies
- 1 bay leaf
- 2 cloves garlic
- ¾ tablespoon salt
- 2 cups water
- 1 teaspoon coconut oil

Directions

1. Push the STEAM button and set the timer to 5 minutes.
2. Add the oil and heat it.
3. Next, stir in the ginger-garlic paste, red chilies, onion, bay leaf and cloves. Sauté them for 4-5 minutes.
4. Then, add in the rest the ingredients.
5. Close the lid and press WHITE RICE and let it cook until the cycle completes.
6. Once the cooker switches to WARM mode, let it sit for 5 minutes.
7. Fluff with a fork and serve!

Nutrition Values (Per Serving)
Calories: 251 Fat: 7g Carbohydrates: 39g Protein: 7g

Potatoes Kale Mix

Servings: 6 | Prep Time: 10 minutes | Cooking Time: 35 minutes

Ingredients

1 cup couscous
2 golden potatoes, diced
9-10 kale leaves, chopped
1 cup vegetable stock
1 teaspoon cumin
1 ½ tablespoon lemon juice
½ teaspoon lemon zest
1 teaspoon parsley
¾ tablespoon salt
½ teaspoon coconut oil

Directions

1. Push the STEAM button and set timer to 40 minutes. Add oil and heat it. Add in the potatoes, couscous, cumin and kale leaves.
2. Sauté for 4-5 minutes. Then, add the rest the ingredients and close the lid.
3. Let them cook for 30-35 minutes. Once the cooking is complete, carefully open the lid stir and serve immediately.

Nutrition Values (Per Serving)

Calories: 548 Fat: 34g Carbohydrates: 38g Protein: 27g

Quinoa Pomegranate Salad

Servings: 4 | Prep Time: 10 minutes| Cooking Time: 35 minutes

Ingredients

2 cups quinoa, rinsed
4 cups water
1 cup pomegranate seeds
½ teaspoon all-spice powder
½ cup fresh mint, chopped

1 tablespoon pine nuts, toasted
Juice from 1 lemon
1 teaspoon olive oil
Salt and pepper to taste

Directions

1. Add quinoa, water and a pinch of salt to your Aroma Cooker. Close the lid, press BROWN RICE, and let the cycle complete.
2. In the meantime, toast the pine nuts over medium heat in a skillet.
3. Once the quinoa is ready, carefully open the lid and add the spice powder and lemon juice. Give it a good stir and let cool.
4. Once cooled, add the pomegranate seeds and pine nuts. Toss and serve!

Nutrition Values (Per Serving)

Calories: 350 Fat: 17g Carbohydrates: 40g Protein: 12g

Healthy Kale Pasta

Servings: 4 | Prep Time: 5 minutes | Cooking Time: 15 minutes

Ingredients

1 ½ cups kale, chopped
1 ½ cups whole wheat pasta
½ cup kidney beans, cooked
3 garlic cloves, minced
1 onion, finely chopped
1 teaspoon oregano
½ teaspoon thyme
Salt and pepper to taste
2 ½ cups water

Directions

1. Add all the above-listed ingredients to your Aroma cooker. Stir well and seal the lid. Push the STEAM button and set the timer to 15 minutes.
2. Carefully open the lid, give it a good stir and serve immediately.

Nutrition Values (Per Serving)

Calories: 242 Fat: 9g Carbohydrates: 31g Protein: 9g

Deliciously Steamed Mac And Cheese

Servings: 3 | Prep Time: 10 minutes | Cooking Time: 40 minutes

Ingredients

- 1 ½ cups elbow macaroni
- 1 ½ cups vegetable broth
- 1 cup unsweetened almond milk
- ¾ cup cheddar cheese, shredded
- ½ cup mozzarella cheese, shredded
- ¼ cup parmesan cheese, grated
- ¼ teaspoon paprika
- Salt and pepper to taste

Directions

1. Add macaroni, broth, almond milk to your Aroma Cooker. Push the STEAM button and set to 40 minutes. Seal the lid and cook until the macaroni are tender.
2. Open the lid and stir in cheeses, salt, paprika and pepper. Give it a good stir.
3. Let steam until the cheese melts. Serve immediately and enjoy.

Nutrition Values (Per Serving)

Calories: 522 Fat: 24g Carbohydrates: 51g Protein: 25g

Subtle "Yellow" Dal

Servings: 4 | Prep Time: 10 minutes | Cooking Time: 20 minutes

Ingredients

- 1 cup chickpea dal
- 1 onion, finely chopped
- 1 onion, thinly sliced
- 4 garlic cloves, minced
- 1 teaspoon cumin powder
- 2 mild green chilies
- 1 teaspoon tamarind paste
- 1 teaspoon olive oil
- 2 cups water

Directions

1. Push the STEAM button and set timer to 10 minutes. Add oil and heat it.
2. Stir in the ginger, garlic, chilies and onion and sauté for 2-3 minutes.
3. Then, add the remaining ingredients and close the lid. Select WHITE RICE and let the cooking cycle to complete.
4. Once it goes off, it will automatically switch to WARM mode. Open the lid and check consistency. Let it sit on WARM for 5 minutes before serving.

Nutrition Values (Per Serving)

Calories: 326 Fat: 10g Carbohydrates: 49g Protein: 14g

Rice Cooker Polenta

Servings: 4 | Prep Time: 5 minutes | Cooking Time: 20 minutes

Ingredients

1 cup cornmeal
3 cups water
¼ cup parmesan cheese, grated
3 green onions, finely chopped
1 tablespoon olive oil
½ teaspoon oregano
½ teaspoon basil
½ teaspoon thyme
¼ teaspoon marjoram
¼ teaspoon sage

Directions

1. Add all the ingredients to your Aroma Rice Cooker, except for parmesan cheese. Close the lid, press the WHITE RICE button, and let the cycle complete.
2. Once the cooker switches to WARM mode, let it sit for 10 minutes, lid closed.
3. Sprinkle with freshly grated parmesan cheese and serve hot!

Nutrition Values (Per Serving)

Calories: 294 Fat: 14g Carbohydrates: 32g Protein: 10g

CHAPTER 4
SOUPS, STEWS AND CHILIES

Exquisite Clam Chowder

Servings: 4-6 | Prep Time: 10 minutes | Cooking Time: 30 minutes

Ingredients

- 2 tablespoons butter
- 1 cup onion, chopped
- 1 cup celery leaves, chopped
- 2 garlic cloves, chopped
- 2 cups fingerling potatoes, cubed
- 1 tablespoon flour
- 2 cups vegetable stock
- 1 cup heavy cream
- 1 can 16 ounce clams, chopped
- 1 bay leaf
- 1 sprig fresh thyme

Directions

1. Push the STEAM button and set timer to 20 minutes.
2. Add butter and melt it.
3. Stir in the onion, garlic and celery and cook for 2-3 minutes.
4. Mix in the flour, and then pour the vegetable stock, bay leaf, sprig thyme and potatoes.
5. Close the lid and let the cycle complete.
6. Open the lid and stir in the cream and chopped clams with juice.
7. Close the lid again and cook for 5 minutes more. Serve warm and enjoy.

Nutrition Values (Per Serving)
Calories: 436 Fat: 20g Carbohydrates: 39g Protein: 27g

Authentic Tortellini Soup

Servings: 6 | Prep Time: 5 minutes | Cooking Time: 20 minutes

Ingredients

2 tablespoons butter
1 white onion, diced
4 cloves garlic, minced
2 tablespoons roasted red pepper, diced
4 cups chicken broth
1 28 ounce can diced tomatoes, with juice
1 15-oz can pinto beans, drained and rinsed
1 cup heavy cream
⅓ cup parmesan cheese, grated
2 tablespoons Italian seasoning
Salt and pepper, to taste
12 ounces refrigerated tortellini
4 large handfuls spinach

Directions

1. Push the STEAM button and set timer to 5 minutes.
2. Once hot, add butter and melt.
3. Stir in onion, garlic, roasted pepper and cook for 2 minutes, until soft and translucent.
4. Add broth, pinto beans, tomatoes, heavy cream, seasoning and cheese.
5. Close the lid and bring it to a simmer. Carefully open the lid and add spinach and tortellini.
6. Let simmer for 10 minutes until the soup thickens.
7. Top with freshly grated parmesan cheese and serve.

Nutrition Values (Per Serving)

Calories: 487 Fat: 26g Carbohydrates: 65g Protein: 34g

Pork and Mushroom Creamy Stew

Servings: 4 | Prep Time: 10 minutes | Cooking Time: 30 minutes

Ingredients

For Grains

4 tablespoons water
4 large asparagus spears, tough ends removed sliced into 1-inch long slivers
1 cup white rice, rinsed and drained
Dash sea salt

For Stew

1 pound pork tenderloin, trimmed with membranes remove and sliced into ¼ inch thick half-moons, rinsed and patted dry using kitchen towel
¼ pound baby carrots, tops remove and skin scrubbed clean, unpeeled
1 can 15-oz whole button mushrooms, small caps, rinsed and drained
1 can 15-oz straw mushrooms, rinsed and drained whole
1 small red bell pepper, deseeded and ribbed, cubed
1 cup sour cream
1 cup mushroom broth
1 teaspoon fish sauce
Salt and pepper to taste
Water
1 tablespoon fresh parsley, minced for garnish

Directions

1. Take a large sheet of aluminum foil and make a pouch with sealed edges.
2. Place all the rice ingredients in the pouch and stir. Seal the edges and set the pouch in a steamer tray.
3. Add all listed stew ingredients to your Aroma Pot, except the sour cream, water and parsley. Pour water until line 3. Place steamer tray in your Cooker.
4. Close the lid and push STEAM button, set timer to 25 minutes.

5. One the cooking cycle completes, turn the cooker off and remove steam steamer tray. Let the pouch cool. Stir well the stew and adjust seasoning.
6. Serve by spooning the stew mix and topping with a portion of the rice and peas mix. Garnish with parsley if needed.

Nutrition Values (Per Serving)

Calories: 462 Fat: 28g Carbohydrates: 14g Protein: 37g

Very Comforting Beef Stew

Servings: 4 | Prep Time: 5 minutes | Cooking Time: 45 minutes

Ingredients

1 pound beef stew meat
½ large potato, diced
½ cup peas
½ medium carrot, diced
12 ounces tomato puree
1 cup celery, diced
½ cup butter bean
2 tablespoons vegetable oil
½ cup water
1 teaspoon garlic, minced
2 tablespoons dry onion soup mix
¼ cup capsicum, diced

Directions

1. Push the STEAM button and set timer to 10 minutes. Pour oil and heat it. Add the beef and cook for 5 minutes until brown.
2. Add the rest of the ingredients and stir well. Seal the lid, press the BROWN RICE button, and let the cooking cycle to complete. Carefully open the lid and serve hot.

Nutrition Values (Per Serving)

Calories: 468 Fat: 23g Carbohydrates: 17g Protein: 46g

Tantalizing Split Pea Soup

Servings: 4 | Prep Time: 5 minutes | Cooking Time: 60 minutes

Ingredients

1 cup yellow split peas
4 cups vegetable broth
½ bay leaf
¼ teaspoon ground coriander seeds
½ tablespoon olive oil
Salt and pepper to taste

Directions

1. Add all ingredients to your Aroma rice cooker and gently stir.
2. Close the lid, push the STEAM button, and set timer to 60 minutes.
3. Once the cooking cycle is over, carefully open the lid and season to taste.
4. Serve and enjoy!

Nutrition Values (Per Serving)

Calories: 360 Fat: 12g Carbohydrates: 49g Protein: 16g

Grand Ma's Chicken Soup

Servings: 4 | Prep Time: 5 minutes | Cooking Time: 20 minutes

Ingredients

2 boneless and skinless chicken breast, diced
4 cups chicken stock
1 yellow onion, diced
2 garlic cloves, minced
1 cup baby spinach
1 carrot, cut into thin rounds
½ cup frozen broccoli
½ cup frozen cauliflower
2 cups egg noodle
½ tablespoon olive oil
Salt to taste

Directions

1. Push the STEAM button and set timer to 20 minutes. Add oil and heat it. Add in onion, garlic, carrots and cook for 2 minutes.
2. Then add the chicken and vegetables and sauté for 6-7 minutes. Next, add the chicken stock and season. Allow the mixture to reach a boil and add the noodles.
3. Cook until the noodles are tender and spinach have wilted. Serve warm.

Nutrition Values (Per Serving)

Calories: 229 Fat: 13g Carbohydrates: 11g Protein: 18g

Extra Creamy Mushroom Soup

Servings: 4 | Prep Time: 5 minutes | Cooking Time: 25 minutes

Ingredients

1 cup button mushrooms, diced
1 white onion, sliced
2 garlic cloves, minced
¼ cup coconut milk
½ cup water
Sea salt and pepper to taste
1 teaspoon coconut oil

Directions

1. Push the STEAM button and set timer to 25 minutes. Add oil and heat it.
2. Then add the garlic, onion and mushrooms and sauté for 2 minutes. Add the rest of the ingredients, except for the coconut milk. Close the lid and cook on STEAM mode for 20 minutes.
3. Once the cooking cycle is complete, open the lid and let the soup cool.
4. Stir in coconut milk and blend the soup using an immersion blender.

Nutrition Values (Per Serving)

Calories: 368 Fat: 9g Carbohydrates: 63g Protein: 10g

A Fine Taco Soup

Servings: 6 | Prep Time: 10 minutes | Cooking Time: 50 minutes

Ingredients

5 cups chicken stock
1 small white onion, diced
1 cup corn kernels
2 carrots, diced small
3 chicken breasts, skinless and boneless, diced
1 12 ounce can diced tomatoes
1 garlic clove, minced
½ cup black beans, rinsed
½ cup brown rice
1 tablespoon olive oil
Salt to taste

Directions

1. Push the STEAM button and set the timer to 10 minutes.
2. Pour the oil and heat it.
3. Add onion and garlic and cook for 2 minutes, or until the onion is translucent.
4. Add the chicken and cook for 5 minutes until brown.
5. Then add the chicken stock, tomatoes, rice, carrots, corn and beans.
6. Close the lid and press the BROWN RICE button, allowing the cooking cycle to complete.
7. Once it goes off, open the lid and serve hot.
8. Serve and enjoy!

Nutrition Values (Per Serving)

Calories: 149 Fat: 4g Carbohydrates: 18g Protein: 12g

Spicy Lemongrass Shrimp Bowl

Servings: 4 | Prep Time: 5 minutes | Cooking Time: 25 minutes

Ingredients

- 1 pound uncooked jumbo shrimp, peeled and deveined
- 2 carrots, sliced diagonally
- 2 celery stalks, sliced diagonally
- ½ onion, sliced diagonally
- 2 cloves garlic, thinly sliced
- 2 large slices fresh ginger
- 2 tablespoons red pepper flakes
- 1 lemongrass stalk
- 4 cups vegetable broth
- 2 tablespoons coconut oil

Directions

1. Prepare the lemongrass by removing the tough outer leaves and cutting the stalk into 2-3 inch pieces.
2. Bruise the stalk by bending them a few times.
3. Push the STEAM button and set timer to 25 minutes.
4. Add in the oil heat it.
5. Then add in the vegetables, ginger, garlic and sauté for 10 minutes, stirring occasionally.
6. Add broth and red pepper flakes, close the lid and cook for 10 minutes.
7. After that, open the lid and add the shrimp.
8. Keep cooking for 2-3 more minutes until the shrimp are barely pink.
9. Serve warm.

Nutrition Values (Per Serving)

Calories: 115 Fat: 1g Carbohydrates: 9g Protein: 17g

Pork and Vegetable Spicy Stew

Servings: 4 | Prep Time: 5 minutes | Cooking Time: 50 minutes

Ingredients

For Rice

4 tablespoon water
1 cup white rice, rinsed and drained

For Stew

1 pound pork belly, sliced into inch thick cubes
¼ pound winged beans, ends removed sliced into inch long slivers
2 pieces large, red ripe tomatoes, quartered
1 piece, large daikon white radish, peeled and sliced into ¼ inch medallions
1 piece medium shallot, peeled and quartered
1 small piece taro, peeled and sliced into inch thick cubes
1 tablespoon tamarind paste
1 teaspoon fish sauce
½ teaspoon black peppercorns
Kosher salt as needed
Water as needed

Directions

1. Take a large sheet of aluminum foil and make a pouch with sealed edges.
2. Pour in water and rice and seal edges.
3. Transfer to a steamer tray.
4. Add the stew ingredients to the Aroma Cooker, except for the water.
5. Add water to line 4. Place the steamer tray on top.
6. Close the lid and push the STEAM button and set timer to 45 minutes.
7. Once the cooking cycle is complete, carefully open the lid and remove the pouch.
8. Let it cool.

9. Stir the stew and adjust the seasoning.
10. Serve by taking the rice from the pouch and dividing it into serving bowls.
11. Ladle 1 portion of the stew on top.

Nutrition Values (Per Serving)

Calories: 224 Fat: 10g Carbohydrates: 25g Protein: 10g

Coolest Rice Beef Soup

Servings: 6 | Prep Time: 10 minutes | Cooking Time: 1 hour 30 minutes

Ingredients

1 ½ cups long-grain rice
10 cups water
1 tablespoon fresh parsley, chopped
1 tablespoon fresh chives, chopped
1 tablespoon fresh rosemary, chopped
Salt and pepper to taste
½ teaspoon cinnamon, ground
2 pounds beef, cubed

Directions

1. Add rice, parsley, water, chives, rosemary and pepper to your Aroma cooker.
2. Close the lid and press WHITE RICE, and cook on the preset amount of time.
3. Once ready, the cooker will switch to WARM mode.
4. Open the lid and add the beef and cinnamon.
5. Stir well and close the lid.
6. Press WHITE RICE again and allow the cooking cycle to complete.
7. Carefully open the lid and serve warm.

Nutrition Values (Per Serving)

Calories: 230 Fat: 7g Carbohydrates: 25g Protein: 17g

Chicken White Radish Soup

Servings: 3 | Prep Time: 10 minutes | Cooking Time: 90 minutes

Ingredients

½ pound chicken breasts, skinless and chopped
5 ginger slices
1 white radish (daikon), peeled and cut to large chunks
8 shiitake mushrooms, stem removed
1 tablespoon wolfberries, soaked until puffy, drained
3 dried scallops
Salt and pepper to taste
5 cups water

Directions

1. Add 2 cups water and fill up to line 2.
2. Press STEAM and set timer to 20 minutes.
3. Once the water starts to boil, add chicken and cook for 8-10 minutes, with the lid closed.
4. Then, discard the water and keep the chicken inside.
5. Add 3 cups of water and cover the chicken pieces.
6. Once the water starts to boil again, add daikon, mushrooms, dried scallops and ginger.
7. Close the lid and press WHITE RICE, let the cycle complete.
8. Once the cooker switches to WARM, let it sit for 1.5-2 hours in WARM mode.
9. About 30 minutes prior to serving, add the soaked wolfberries.
10. Season and enjoy!

Nutrition Values (Per Serving)

Calories: 345 Fat: 19g Carbohydrates: 38g Protein: 8g

A Fine Vegetable Stew

Servings: 4 | Prep Time: 5 minutes | Cooking Time: 25 minutes

Ingredients

1 Napa cabbage, cut into 2-inch slices
1 ½ cups warm water
1 teaspoon oyster sauce
3 ounces mung bean, soaked in water for 5 minutes
2 teaspoons brown sugar
1 tablespoon salted soybeans, mashed
8 ounces white mushrooms, sliced
10 ounces tofu, cut into slices
Salt and pepper to taste

Directions

1. In a mid-size bowl, add sugar, oyster sauce, ½ of cup water, and mix well.
2. Press the STEAM button and set the timer to 25 minutes.
3. Add oil to the rice cooker and heat it.
4. Add the mashed soy beans and cook for 3 minutes.
5. Then add the rest the ingredients and close the lid. Cook for 17-20 minutes.
6. Once the cooking is over, carefully open the lid and adjust the seasoning.
7. Serve hot.

Nutrition Values (Per Serving)

Calories: 468 Fat: 21g Carbohydrates: 66g Protein: 19g

Healthy Veggie Lentil Soup

Servings: 8 | Prep Time: 5 minutes | Cooking Time: 50 minutes

Ingredients

- 8 ounces fire roasted tomatoes
- 2 carrots, diced
- 6 cups vegetable broth
- ¼ teaspoon ground coriander seeds
- 1 tablespoon olive oil
- 8 ounces brown lentils, rinsed
- 2 celery stalks, chopped
- ¼ teaspoon ground cumin
- Salt and pepper to taste

Directions

1. Add the listed ingredients to your Aroma Cooker. Give it a good stir.
2. Push the STEAM button and set timer to 50 minutes. Allow the mixture to reach simmer, with the lid open. Then close the lid and let the STEAM cycle to complete. Once done, carefully Open the lid and season to taste.

Nutrition Values (Per Serving)

Calories: 268 Fat: 1g Carbohydrates: 50g Protein: 17g

Fascinating Rice Chili Stew

Servings: 6 | Prep Time: minute | Cooking Time: 25 minutes

Ingredients

- ½ cup white rice
- ¼ cup cooked black beans
- ¼ cup sweet corn
- 1 garlic clove, minced
- 1 teaspoon ginger paste
- 1 teaspoon cumin powder
- 1 teaspoon chili pepper
- 1 teaspoon oregano
- 1 avocado, sliced
- 1 teaspoon lemon juice
- 1 ½ cups water

Directions

1. Add all the listed ingredients to your Aroma cooker except for the avocado and lemon juice.
2. Close the lid, press the STEAM button, and set timer to 25 minutes.
3. Once the cycle is complete, carefully open the lid and drizzle lemon juice.
4. Serve topped with sliced avocados and enjoy!

Nutrition Values (Per Serving)

Calories: 306 Fat: 9g Carbohydrates: 45g Protein: 14g

Lentils Kale Miso Soup

Servings: 6 | Prep Time: 10 minutes | Cooking Time: 20 minutes

Ingredients

½ cup lentils
7-8 kale leaves, chopped
¼ cup sweet corn
1 tablespoon Miso paste
1 teaspoon sea salt
1 garlic clove, minced
½ teaspoon pepper powder
1 cup water

Directions

1. Add all the listed ingredients to your Aroma cooker.
2. Push the STEAM button and set timer to 20 minutes.
3. Close the lid and let the cooking cycle complete.
4. Once done, carefully open the lid and stir. Serve the soup hot and enjoy!

Nutrition Values (Per Serving)

Calories: 256 Fat: 8g Carbohydrates: 45g Protein: 8g

CHAPTER 5
DESSERTS

Corn Plantains A la Coconut Rice

Servings: 4 | Prep Time: 5 minutes | Cooking Time: 25 minutes

Ingredients

5 small over ripe plantains, peeled

For Rice

2 tablespoons plain sugar, crumbled
3 cups white rice, rinsed
¼ cup bottled jackfruit in syrup, lightly drained, minced
1 can 15-oz coconut cream
1 can 15-oz whole corn kernels
Dash kosher salt

Directions

1. Place plantains in a steamer tray. Set aside.
2. Add the rice mix ingredients to your Aroma cooker except for ½ can of coconut cream. Stir and pour water until line 4.
3. Place steamer rack on top and close the lid.
4. Push the WHITE RICE button and let cooking cycle complete and reach WARM mode.
5. Carefully open the lid and drain the plantains.
6. Slice them into ¼ inch medallions.
7. Season the rice and serve with sliced plantains and drizzle coconut cream.

Nutrition Values (Per Serving)

Calories: 259 Fat: 9g Carbohydrates: 42g Protein: 5g

Children's Favorite Banana Pudding

Servings: 2 | Prep Time: 10 minutes | Cooking Time: 90 minutes

Ingredients

- 1 cup self-rising flour
- 2 tablespoons whole milk
- ½ teaspoon cinnamon, ground
- 1 medium-sized egg, lightly whisked
- 1 sliced banana + 2 extra mashed bananas
- 2 tablespoons brown sugar + ⅓ cup extra
- 3 ounces butter

Directions

1. Grease the inner pot of your Aroma Cooker and line with parchment paper.
2. Drizzle 1 ounce of butter on top and sprinkle with 2 tablespoons brown sugar.
3. Lay the slices of 1 banana on top and set the pot aside.
4. Take a bowl and add the remaining brown sugar and butter, the cinnamon, egg, milk, mashed bananas and mix well. Stir in the flour.
5. Fold this mixture gently over the bananas in your Rice Cooker.
6. Close the lid and press STEAM, set timer to 5 minutes and cook until the cooking cycle is over.
7. Let warm for 10 minutes, then press STEAM again and adjust the timer to 3 minutes.
8. Once the cycle is complete, it will automatically switch to WARM. Let it rest for 10 more minutes.
9. Keep repeating this process until a toothpick comes out clean from the center.
10. Once ready, transfer the pudding onto a plate and discard baking paper.
11. Serve and enjoy!

Nutrition Values (Per Serving)

Calories: 512 Fat: 26g Carbohydrates: 78g Protein: 7g

Mesmerizing Wine-Poached Caramelized Pears

Servings: 4 | Prep Time: 5 minutes | Cooking Time: 12 minutes

Ingredients

- 2 cups sweet dessert wine
- 2 large pears, halved and cored
- ½ a teaspoon ground nutmeg
- ¼ cup premium caramel sauce
- Whipped cream for garnish

Directions

1. Pour wine into the inner pot your Aroma Cooker. Add nutmeg and stir.
2. Add pears, cut side facing down in a steamer tray and place the steamer tray in the Cooker.
3. Close the lid and push the STEAM button, set timer to 12 minutes. Let the cooking cycle complete.
4. Serve by placing one half the pear on a dessert plate and drizzling the caramel sauce on top. Toss a dollop of whipped cream on top and enjoy!

Nutrition Values (Per Serving)

Calories: 354 Fat: 14g Carbohydrates: 51g Protein: 2g

Golden Butter Cake

Servings: 8 | Prep Time: 5 minutes | Cooking Time: 25 minutes

Ingredients

- 2 cups all-purpose flour
- 2 teaspoons baking powder
- 2 eggs, beaten
- 1 ½ cups milk
- 1 teaspoon orange zest
- 2 tablespoons honey
- 1 teaspoon vanilla paste

Directions

1. Take a bowl and whisk flour and baking powder. Add eggs, vanilla and orange zest. Gradually mix in with the milk.
2. Once the ingredients are well incorporated, grease the inner pot of your Aroma Cooker and pour the batter.
3. Press STEAM and set the timer to 25 minutes. Seal the lid and let the cooking cycle complete.
4. Then carefully remove the lid. Slice the cake and serve warm.

Nutrition Values (Per Serving)

Calories: 300 Fat: 13g Carbohydrates: 41g Protein: 4g

Warm Rice Pudding

Servings: 6 | Prep Time: 5 minutes | Cooking Time: 30 minutes

Ingredients

⅔ cup Arborio Rice
¼ cup sugar
1 teaspoon vanilla paste

1 teaspoon lemon zest
4 cups milk
1 egg

Directions

1. Add rice and milk to your Rice Cooker.
2. Seal the lid and press WHITE RICE. Cook until the preset time is over.
3. In the meantime, in a bowl, whisk in the eggs, sugar and lemon zest.
4. Once the cooking is over, carefully open the lid and stir in the egg mixture in a steady stream. Close the lid and press STEAM button, and set to 15 minutes.
5. Carefully open the lid and divide the mixture among serving bowls.

Nutrition Values (Per Serving)

Calories: 135 Fat: 5g Carbohydrates: 20g Protein: 4g

Tapioca Coconut Stew

Servings: 6 | Prep Time: 10 minutes | Cooking Time: 50 minutes

Ingredients

1 sheet fresh banana leaf, scrubbed well, pat dry with kitchen towels
¼ cup sticky rice, rinsed and drained
Dash kosher salt

For Stew

1 small unpeeled purple yam
1 small plantain, overripe, peeled and diced
1 small sweet potato, peeled and diced
1 small piece taro, peeled and diced
1 can 15-oz coconut cream
½ cup palm sugar, crumbled
¼ cup cooked large tapioca pears, rinsed and drained
¼ cup cooked small tapioca pearls, rinsed and drained
¼ cup bottled jackfruit in syrup, drained and julienned
Water as needed

Directions

1. Place unpeeled yam in a deep saucepan and pour water to submerge the yam.
2. Place the pan on high heat and let the water come to a boil. Remove from heat.
3. Place the lid and let the yam sit in the boiled water for 1 hour.
4. Drain and cool the yam. Then peel and dice into bite-sized portions.
5. Take a ramekin and line it with strips of banana leaves.
6. Place rice into ramekin and season with salt. Place in your steam tray.
7. Add the rice ingredients to your rice cooker except for the water and ½ of the coconut cream. Give it a good stir. Pour water until line 3.
8. Close the lid and press BROWN RICE. Cook until the preset cycle is over and it goes to WARM mode. Remove the lid and the steamer tray.

9. Fluff the rice and discard banana leaves. Add remaining coconut cream into the stew and give it a good stir. Enjoy!

Nutrition Values (Per Serving)

Calories: 513 Fat: 29g Carbohydrates: 74g Protein: 3g

Astonishingly Black Sesame Cake

Servings: 6 | Prep Time: 10 minutes | Cooking Time: 60-65 minutes

Ingredients

1 cup all-purpose flour (sifted)
4 large eggs (yolks separated)
½ cup sugar
¼ cup ground black sesame seeds
4 tablespoons soy milk
½ tablespoon sesame oil
2-3 drops vanilla extract
1 tablespoon butter

Directions

1. Grease the inner pot your Aroma cooker with butter.
2. Take a bowl and beat egg whites, gradually adding sugar, until stiff.
3. Add yolks, vanilla extract and beat until you obtain a thick mixture.
4. Add flour, ground black sesame seeds and soy milk.
5. Mix well using a rubber spatula. Stir in sesame oil.
6. Pour the batter into your inner pot and tap the bottom to release any air.
7. Close the lid and press STEAM mode, set time for 60 minutes.
8. Once the cooking cycle is complete, carefully open the lid.
9. Serve cooled.

Nutrition Values (Per Serving)

Calories: 294 Fat: 15g Carbohydrates: 37g Protein: 6g

Glazing Chocolate Cake

Servings: 12 | Prep Time: 5 minutes | Cooking Time: 1 hour 5 minutes

Ingredients

1 ½ cups white flour
½ cup raw sugar
4 tablespoons dark cocoa
1 teaspoon baking soda
½ teaspoon salt
½ teaspoon cinnamon
¼ teaspoon double-acting baking powder
½ teaspoon vanilla
1 tablespoon vinegar
1 cup water
¼ cup sunflower oil

Directions

1. Take a bowl and add all the dry ingredients.
2. Mix well and add the wet ingredients to the mixture.
3. Give it a good stir until you have obtained a nice batter.
4. Grease the inner pot your Aroma Cooker and pour the batter.
5. Close the lid and press STEAM. Set the timer to 60 minutes.
6. Once the cooking cycle is over, open the lid and check the center using a toothpick.
7. If it comes out clean, let the cake cool for 15 minutes.
8. Remove it and place it on a serving dish.
9. Sprinkle with powdered sugar and enjoy!

Nutrition Values (Per Serving)

Calories: 280 Fat: 19g Carbohydrates: 27g Protein: 3g

Happy Go Lucky Coconut Rice Pudding

Servings: 6 | Prep Time: 5 minutes | Cooking Time: 1 hour 5 minutes

Ingredients

- 2 cups Arborio rice
- 2 cups cold water
- 1 teaspoon salt
- ½ cup evaporated milk
- ½ cup coconut milk
- 1 cup sweetened condensed milk
- 1 cinnamon stick
- 1 lemon zest, 1 large piece lemon peel
- ½ teaspoon nutmeg
- 3 tablespoons ground cinnamon

Directions

1. Rinse the rice in cold water and drain.
2. Add it to your Aroma Cooker. Season with salt and give it a good stir.
3. Close the lid and press WHITE RICE button.
4. Cook until the preset cycle is over.
5. Open the lid and stir gently. Let cool for 15 minutes.
6. Take a bowl and add the evaporated milk, sweetened condensed milk, cinnamon stick, lemon zest, nutmeg and stir.
7. Pour the mixture over the rice.
8. Cover and set on WARM setting to simmer for 30 minutes.
9. Keep checking the consistency and discard cinnamon stick and lemon zest after 10 minutes.
10. Once ready, garnish with cream and ground cinnamon, and serve.

Nutrition Values (Per Serving)

Calories: 488 Fat: 38g Carbohydrates: 56g Protein: 7g

Poached Pomegranate with Spiced Pears

Servings: 4 | Prep Time: 5 minutes + poach and chill time | Cooking Time: 2h

Ingredients

2 firm pears, peeled, halved and cored
2 cups pomegranate juice
2 cups apple cider
1-3 inch cinnamon stick peel from one clementine
2 whole cloves
2-star anise
3 black cardamom pods
1 1-inch fresh ginger, peeled and cut into thin slivers

Directions

1. Add pomegranate juice, apple cider, cinnamon stick, clementine peel, star anise, cloves, cardamom pods and ginger to your Aroma cooker.
2. Poach the pear halves in your desired poaching liquid and place them in the Rice Cooker.
3. Close the lid and press STEAM. Set the timer to 50 minutes.
4. Once the cooking is complete, open the lid and check with a toothpick until it goes easily through.
5. Let the pears rest for 1 hour (not cook), turn them over and let them sit for another hour.
6. If you want a more intense flavor, chill them in the fridge overnight.

Nutrition Values (Per Serving)

Calories: 187 Fat: 13g Carbohydrates: 20g Protein: 1g

The Ever So Popular Sticky Mango Rice

Servings: 2 | Prep Time: 10 minutes | Cooking Time: 35 minutes

Ingredients

1 tablespoon mung beans, toasted
½ teaspoon flour, rice
⅓ teaspoon salt
3 tablespoons coconut sugar
1 Mango, sliced
½ cup full fat coconut milk
1 cup sticky rice

Directions

1. Add the rice to your Aroma cooker and press the STEAM button.
2. Set timer to 30 minutes, close the lid and STEAM the rice until tender.
3. Meanwhile, take a pan and place it over medium heat. Add coconut sugar and milk and let the sugar dissolve, for a few minutes.
4. Once the rice is steamed, take it out and transfer to a bowl.
5. Pour ¾ of the coconut milk and sugar mixture on top and give it a good stir.
6. Let it sit for 20 minutes.
7. Add ½ a teaspoon rice flour to the remaining coconut milk and heat it until thick.
8. Divide the sticky rice amongst serving bowls and top with thick coconut milk. Sprinkle mung beans on top and serve with mango slices.

Nutrition Values (Per Serving)

Calories: 576 Fat: 13g Carbohydrates: 110g Protein: 7g

Rose Pudding

Servings: 6 | Prep Time: 10 minutes | Cooking Time: 30 minutes

Ingredients

1 cup soaked rice
1 cup almond milk
¼ teaspoon cardamom powder
½ teaspoon rose essence
1 teaspoon olive oil

Directions

1. Set on STEAM mode and set timer to 30 minutes.
2. Pour the oil and heat it. Add the rice and sauté it for 6 minutes.
3. Add the remaining ingredients to the pot, except for the rose essence. Close the lid and cook until the preset cooking time is over.
4. Carefully open the lid and stir in rose essence.
5. Serve and enjoy!

Nutrition Values (Per Serving)

Calories: 189 Fat: 1g Carbohydrates: 41g Protein: 5g

Coconut Pecan "Upside Down" Cake

Servings: 4 | Prep Time: 5 minutes | Cooking Time: 45 minutes

Ingredients

½ cup butter, soft
½ cup dark brown sugar
½ cup coconut, shredded
⅔ cup pecans, chopped
½ cup semi-sweet chocolate
2 tablespoons milk
1 (9 ounce) box yellow cake mix

Directions

1. Grease the inner pot your Aroma cooker with cooking spray.
2. In a bowl, add brown sugar, coconut, pecan, chocolate and 1 tbsp of milk. Mix well.
3. Spread the butter and mix up cake mix according to the package instructions.
4. Pour the batter into your greased Rice Cooker and seal the lid.
5. Press STEAM and set timer to 40 minutes. Once the cooking cycle is over, let it sit for 5 minutes. Then, carefully take the inner pot out and let it cool.
6. Serve the cake cooled.

Nutrition Values (Per Serving)

Calories: 545 Fat: 37g Carbohydrates: 76g Protein: 4g

Astonishing Rice Cooker Walnut Cake

Servings: 6 | Prep Time: 10 minutes | Cooking Time: 35 minutes

Ingredients

1 tablespoon maple sugar
½ cup walnuts
1 ½ cups water
2 cups pancake mix

Directions

1. Take a bowl and add pancake mix and water. Stir gently.
2. Add walnuts, stir again. Pour this mixture into your Aroma Cooker and sprinkle maple sugar on top.
3. Close the lid, press BROWN RICE button and cook until the preset cycle is over. Open the lid and check using a tooth pick for doneness. Serve chilled.

Nutrition Values (Per Serving)

Calories: 350 Fat: 23g Carbohydrates: 30g Protein: 6g

Sensible Apple Rice Pudding

Servings: 4 | Prep Time: 20 minutes | Cooking Time: 40 minutes

Ingredients

2 cups apples, peeled, cored and diced
1 cup short grain white rice
3 cups water
½ teaspoon salt
1 cup raisins
1 pinch nutmeg
1 can 14 ounce sweetened condensed milk
4 tablespoons butter
1 ½ tablespoon vanilla

Directions

1. Add rice, water, raisins, apple and nutmeg to your Rice Cooker.
2. Seal the lid and press the WHITE RICE button. Cook until the preset cooking cycle is over.
3. Once the cooker switches to WARM, open the lid and stir in condensed milk, vanilla and butter.
4. Close the lid again and press STEAM.
5. Cook to 15 minutes until the pudding is set.

Nutrition Values (Per Serving)

Calories: 424 Fat: 16g Carbohydrates: 69g Protein: 5g

CONCLUSION

I can't express how honored I am to think that you found my book interesting and informative enough to read it all through to the end.

I thank you again for purchasing this book and I hope that you had as much fun reading it as I had writing it.

I bid you farewell and encourage you to move forward with your amazing Aroma Cooker journey.

Made in the USA
Monee, IL
14 December 2020